Bottom Dog Press

# The Big Book of Daniel*

## The Collected Poems of Daniel Thompson

Edited by Maj Ragain

Bottom Dog Press
Huron, Ohio

Bottom Dog Press
PO Box 425/ Huron, OH 33829
http://smithdocs.net
**lsmithdog@smithdocs.net**

**Credits:**
General editor Larry Smith
Book editor Maj Ragain
Cover design by Susanna Sharp-Schwacke
Cover Photos:
Front by Jim Lang
Back by Janet Century
Other Photos:
Page 21 Daniel at 1985 Junkyard Reading
Page 93 Daniel in police booking shot, 1961
Page 207 Daniel with children, c. 1961
Page 253 Daniel at Lakewood Library, 2004 by Jim Lang
Page 333 Daniel with dogs, by Margo Brown

**Acknowledgements**
We thank the William C. Wright Trust for support.

*Famous in the Neighborhood*, Burning Press, Luigi-Bob
    Drake, editor, Cleveland, Ohio, 1988.
*Even the Broken Letters of the Heart Spell Earth*, Bottom Dog
    Press, Larry Smith, editor, Huron, Ohio, 1998
    (includes a CD of the author reading, accompanied by
    Ernie Krivda on saxphone and Bill DeArango on guitar).
*Comforting the Dead*, Green Panda Press, Bree, editor, 2004.
*The Rain Poet*, Green Panda Press, Bree, editor, 2004.
*Double X*, Jim Lang, publisher, 2004.
Over the decades, more than one hundred of Daniel's
poems have been published in *Artcrimes,* Steven B. Smith,
editor.

Additional acknowledgements may be found on page 339.

Many helped in bringing these poems to print: LuAnn Csernotta, Bill Kennedy, Jim Lang, Kay Thompson, Tim Joyce, Barbara Klonowski, Barry Zucker, Flo Cunningham, Marianne Riggenbach, Larry Smith, and others, among the countless friends of Daniel.

Dedicated to Barbara Klonowski

**The Big Book of Daniel**

**Section One "O Hear My Broken Prayer"**

**Section Two "And the Heart Still Shining, Sings"**

# Foreword

The poet Antonio Machado dreamed of a beehive inside his chest where golden bees *made sweet honey from my old failures.* It is what poets do: distill experience into something essential to us all. Daniel has left us the honey of his days, what he gathered in his sixty nine years, the poems which he was still revising up until the final week when the shadows gathered him, May 6, 2004, acute myelogenous leukemia. He had been diagnosed two years earlier. He mustered his courage and remaining strength and continued to spread his words like seeds, in the time allotted him, even traveling to Europe in May, 2002, to perform with the percussion group Drumplay. On his sixty ninth birthday, April 21st, Daniel's life was celebrated by a crowd of friends at the Algebra Tea House in Cleveland's Little Italy. His death, like his life, was a public event. He gave himself away to friend after friend. When death came for him a few weeks after that, there was little left to be taken. Here was a man who, as Whitman said of himself, was *not contained between his hat and his boots.* Daniel's last gift to us, his life's work, over three hundred pages of poems, is the big jug of honey you have in your hands. Taste and see.

A life. Daniel was born on Easter Sunday, April 21, 1935, in Washington, D.C. The Thompsons lived on the West Side of Cleveland where Daniel spent his boyhood. He and his sister Kay attended St. Luke's Lutheran school while his father Howard went off to war and his mother Kathryn worked in a bomber factory. Both parents were union activist New Deal Democrats; the issues of social justice and politics were always in the air. Daniel entered the struggle early. And so it was with poetry. His sister Kay has a vivid recollection of Daniel composing his first poem—at the age of seven—sitting on the front porch of their house in Tremont, offering up his words to the man in the moon. At thirteen Daniel was sent to a Lutheran high school in Fort Wayne, Indiana, and, after graduating, on to Concordia Seminary near St. Louis, for a brief time. In these years away from home, loneliness became his familiar companion and remained with him the rest of his life, a thread running through his poetry. He returned to Cleveland in 1955, attended Fenn College, taught school in Parma and continued to write poems. Daniel eventually graduated from Kent State University with a BA in English and Philosophy, 1966. During those following years Daniel became more and more disenchanted with institutions— religions, governments. As his sister Kay put it, *he lost his faith.* His convictions grew toward those of Gandhi and Martin Luther King, principles of non-violent dissent, changing the world one person at a time. And though he once told his friend Barry Zucker, *I turned to poetry to get those biblical passages out of my head*, it didn't work. That language is deeply embedded in his poems. He found causes on every hand. The poems tell these stories, how he became both the town crier and the people's pastor of the streets, famous in many neighborhoods around Cleveland. His mother had wanted Daniel to become a missionary, and so he was that, with the city as his church.

In 1959 he hitchhiked to San Francisco and found himself at the epicenter of the Beat Generation, its new energy, its freedom. And it marked the beginnings of his involvement with poetry readings which became the main conduit between his private life and his public life for the next thirty five years, the place where the two lives converged. He discovered and become steeped in the poetry of Dylan Thomas and William Butler Yeats. He once remarked that reading Yeats' *The Second Coming* gave him his vision of a poet's life.

He was a poet/social activist all his life. He ranged far and near. He stood up for the homeless, the dispossessed. He gave them their daily bread, donated by local bakeries. He sought out the hungry on the streets and stocked the pantry at Saint Herman's. He founded shelters for battered women, along with many other desperate characters who had his number. Daniel also protested nuclear armament in the 1950s; in 1961 he was a freedom rider, jailed in Jackson, Mississippi, then sent to Parchman Farm, a state prison; he was jailed nineteen times, mostly in the South.

He marched alongside Dr. Martin Luther King. He once caught a brick thrown at Dr. King in Gage Park in 1966. He made the March on Washington in 1963; he was a soldier in the Armies of the Night Pentagon sit-in/shut-down in 1967. He protested the building of a gymnasium on the site of the May 4th shootings at Kent State where he was arrested. In the early 70s, he was charged with jaywalking in Coventry, Cleveland Heights, during a police crackdown on street people, which led to a $430 fine and a three month stay in the Warrensville Workhouse. He took the case to the U.S. Supreme Court and lost. At the Workhouse, he become a counselor and started a program to enable inmates to make bail. He read poems there and taught poetry writing workshops. He picketed Jacob's Field and wrote a poem protesting the Cleveland Indians' Chief Wahoo logo. He contributed to and hawked copies of the *Homeless Grapevine* to raise money for those who slept on grates and wandered the city. He lay down, along with over one hundred others in Cleveland Public Square, in 1985, to protest the nuclear arms race. His poem *Ground Zero: Downtown Cleveland* frames that moment—a die-in, a teach-in, *As down I lied to tell the truth/to save the world.* Daniel was not afraid to be held in the fire.

In 1992 he was proclaimed the poet laureate of Cuyahoga County. The resolution states: *Daniel R. Thompson has distinguished himself as one of Cuyahoga County's most colorful, talented and concerned citizens.* So he was, but that is public speak. The poems tell us much more, and they crack open something hidden deep within us. *Only this, to awake to dream/Can take us beyond our nostalgia for the new/And teach our children how poets live/mouth to mouth, hand to mouth, silent as light.*

Daniel was often on the road, hitchhiking or tooling along in one old beater after another, but always Cleveland was the heart of it all. He wanted the private lives of the poets to be expressed in the public life of the city. He lobbied for Cleveland streets to be named after Hart Crane and Langston Hughes in the hope that doing so would, in his words, *humanize the city.* Faithful to his union organizer beginnings—his mother was once fired from her bomber plant job for doing just that—Daniel founded Cleveland Poetsbank, the legendary Junkstock Readings at Pearl Road Auto Wrecking, Readings In The Flats, the annual Hessler Street Fair and countless other poetry events over the decades. Thoreau, in *Walden,* proposes that poetry is a means by which a place comes to contemplate its own nature. Read these poems, and you come to know much about the body and spirit of Cleveland, as well as that of Daniel.

Daniel had what Robert Frost called *a lover's quarrel with the world,* as well as with his country and his *Comeback City,* Cleveland. He was also the word clown, kneading the playdough of language (Daniel was voted class clown in his senior year of high school). We hear the snap, crackle and pop of his wit playing against the weight of the world. Find his signature poem *Fruits and Vegetables,* memorialized on a plaque outside the West Side Market. So often that wit, coupled with his fearless nature, diffused and disarmed the forces he was pitted against, a relationship, a confrontation, an angry crowd. Some of his most memorable poems come out of the quarrel with himself, that dark honey, tinged with the metallic taste of loss, the old wars of the heart—*the story of how he fell/in with the tigers of wrath/along the road of excess/and dreams now of moon/and shadow, truth and sorrow!* Daniel speaks to the paradox of our shared loneliness. *And our need to break bread/for that sound breaks the silence between us/And out of that broken silence tumbles everything.* Everything. Break the silence. Break the fast. Daniel has arrived with the bread.

On May 6, 2005, the first anniversary of Daniel's death, the street once known as West Second was officially designated Daniel's Way, just off Public Square. It is a short street; it was a long and full life. Some rainy day, walk Daniel's Way. Take this book with you. Find the poem *The Rain Poet.* Read it aloud, quietly.

## The Rain Poet

Save
My poems
For rainy
Days. Say
Them out
Loud. Listen
The rain
Applauds...

Listen to the small hands of the rain. Remember Daniel.

Maj Ragain
January 25, 2011


## The Poems of Daniel


Daniel with the star over his eye
crossing the midnight of many rivers—
cleaves the heart of ten thousand raindrops
offering up small flowers of blackened sunlight
seeking the dark God of the Underground,
singing psalms to strange brothers and sisters
of the even more perfectly wounded and strange.
And any old phrase will never do enough
so he walks the flat and lonesome Midwest miles
in high top mule shoes and workhouse blues
knocking soft rhymes upon the worst of your dreams.
O Sweetheart won't you ever, ever open up?
His tea warm tears color your own rainbows.
Hike up your cloudy skies and let his hunger in.

Tim Joyce

# One

## "O Hear My Broken Prayer"

## Morning Comes Alive

Morning comes alive as bread
Our sidedoor manna fresh from the Israelite
With sinister affection for the enemy
And love of Indians and cigars

Dead thunderbolts, tears in ashes
Entitle one to disability's privilege
As I learned heart to heart
In the halfway house
From the fox as crazy as a fox

Deep in the manure natural to our time
At the root of Liberty's tree
The man who exposes himself
Is full of piss and vinegar
While that trespasser Mesmerized by Pygmalion
Beats on the wall, demanding a polygraph

Each generation casts its own hue
But the source of light is the same
The struggle to be free

O sweet is the chariot
On my tow chain-of-love
Sing the hands of a moustache out of control
On a snuggle of wigs out of the west
In a shoplifter's bag upon the floor
Night falls: the apples of sorrow
Are devoured by the teeth's haha

Here is the latest news
From the land of smoke and dream
Poet climbs tree
Helps hang President in effigy
Says Poet, We are not alone
And our poems will shake
Old Rockefeller's bones

## The Bread Man

Night is the future
I drive in the middle of
Under the weather of moonlight
Under the charity of darkness
With Godspeed I drive
Through the scarred wilderness
The ruderal loneliness
As if I were Heaven's messenger
And had the divine right of way
Across avenues of bad news
To these streets of greed
Night is the future
For the fugitives of day
Who lay their heads down
Where their feet have trod
And hold in rough hands
This day-old daily bread
In a prison without walls
Under stars they seldom see
Night is the future
A dream of a blind date
Our faith arranges
Between justice and love
Under the weather of moonlight
Under the charity of darkness

## Dark Laughter
*for Crow Dog*


Turning at the graffito
To die of a rose
On the wall near the bridge
Where the rapid runs
By Little Italy
The rose having returned
After a short-lived itch
I confront
In the middle of the road
Ready to strike
Escaped no doubt
From last night's flick
By Indian Satyajit Ray
A broken tree-branch cobra
No lightning has snaked this tree
A drought is upon us
To die of a rose, of love
Or the thirst for beauty...
Jesus, it's hot
A heat wave drowns us
In the high nineties
Or has it broken
A hundred, Crow Dog?
Crow Dog's come in black
Red and yellow
With his ancient smoking pipe
His whistle carved
From the bone of an eagle
His dancers in full regalia
To Sherwood Anderson's
Ancestral Ground
Stolen from his ancestors
You're our native hope, Crow Dog
To visit the deep being of our dreams
To reverse the Nazarene
To wed us to the land
Restoring order to nature

Turning the wine of Winesburg
Into water
Into the dark laughter of rain

## Hunger

Uneasy sky
The stars burdened
By our wishes
Below
An ordinary seaman
Of little faith
And new found
Liberty
Falls through
The waves of desire
To the uncharted
Darkness ashore
There
Young men
Whitman would
Have loved
Old companions, too
Veterans of the rain
With more tattoos
Than teeth
And all of us
Fed on irony and dream
Who've rubbed shoulders
With the shadows
Of our fathers
In lieu of loaves
And fishes
Eat Baby Ruth candy bars
On the desolate
Streets of Duluth
This
After a lighthouse
Soul service in which
Guitar player tells
Sins of his youth
Drank, ran around
Wanted by the law
Till he found salvation

Sweet in the verse
*Make a joyful noise*
*Unto the Lord,* then we
Toothless in a nation
Armed to the teeth
Got chocolate from Jesus
Walking the sea
Testing the waters
With this
Ordinary seaman
Of little faith
And new found
Liberty
Who waits
Not for Heaven
But the workers
To strike
Who hungers
To be home
From the sea

## Famous in the Neighborhood

Famous in the neighborhood
Among children and gods
And all living things hidden
I walk about talking nonsense
Inhaling through the ears energy
Putting humor on the mouth showing teeth
In the street I run amuck
Having learned in my quest
For maximum security
A flair for fair play
Everything truly amazes me
How people get up, go to work
How they get through the day
Without breaking down
How at night their dreams let them sleep
Ah, citizens, shopkeepers, servants of the law
This is, indeed, an age of obscenities
The four-letter word has long been outstripped
By its competition from the Pentagon
Pollution is reaching eclipse proportions
We are left muttering to ourselves
Traditional graffiti
And pity poor protest
Bound. Gagged. Held in contempt
Mediocrity sits in the judgment seat
The mad bombers are on the way...
Yet, the rain falls, the grass is wet
The robin eats the worm
The voices of children are heard from the turtle
In the sandbox in the park
As the sun, still famous in my neighborhood
Shines its shoes and walks through the sky

## Desperate Characters

Desperate characters
Shoot their arrows
Straight into my heart
Seduced, I start to bleed
I cannot leave nor stand
Apart from another's weather
We are one together in each
Raindrop of pain, each cloud
Lining's silver flash
Out of their emergency I
Emerge and sigh to their
Every wish, dream and lie
Every rose I stop and smell
Through their broken nose
Desperate characters
Have my number, disturb
My slumber, never let me be
Alone, ring my bell, my phone
Any hour, voices call, draw
Me out, dare me to care, to
Yes, sail my heart again
Into their wild darkness

## Night Poem

Who threads these silences
With weather's fragility
Rails against star, feather and tree
Through the needle's eye
Eyes the pitch of forty elusive winks
In the alphabet of night
Where I's shine forth insomnia
The dreamless ego like a shell-shocked snail
Drags about its own private hell
The smell and then the taste of rain
If only things would happen again
If only I would write again
Lightning strikes; a leaf falls
The grief-stricken tree splits apart
Resembling this schizoid poet
Who also barks when pissed on
And has now—star, bird
Would enough for fiery verse

## The Birds

My machine off
In dream weather
Green everywhere
Turned inward
Counterclockwise
To the eye of the vortex
Before the walled city
Of the fabled warlord
Made an anachronism
By the new regime
There, where some
Stand like statues, I
Listen: the high heart's
Ambient cry

## Lost Days

Lost days, occasionally one
Then another...and another
More often and closer together
Like a woman's pain in labor
Sometimes stupor, sometimes
Delicious sleep, languor
Let me languish
Never get dressed
If I don't wish or washed
No, no clothes
Oh, save a torn bathrobe
Barefoot I'll wander
Room to room, sleep
Anywhere, rest anytime
Night and day
Day turning into
That coal-black porter
Night
Night carrying in its soul
The fire of day, watch
Look, is it A.M.? P.M.?
Hard to tell in the dark
The light from the window
Now moving on the water
In the bath, sleep, dream
Drown in dreams, wake up
Have to get up, get dressed
Get out before it's too late
Before it's here, the big sleep
Death
Is it just a string of lost days
A dream's breath away and then
Heaven, that coup de grace
To break the fast of darkness?

## Adam and Eve in Cleveland

Banished from the garden
Books in hand, Adam and maiden
Eve and man, wander the streets of Cleveland
Their only guide this newfound knowledge of good and evil
It was good in the garden, says Adam
It was evil we had to leave, says Eve
And from passers-by comes a flyleaf of sympathy
To cover their naked grief. Where can they seek relief?
Let's take our sorrow to the river, says Adam
Let the waters wash away our tears
But who's that with the lean and hungry face
Who's stolen, er, borrowed the Cuyahoga's last green space?
Get away, you loafers, says Stouffer's
And Adam and Eve, feeling deceived again, grieve again
O Adam, cries Eve
There seems to be a dearth of nature on earth
It seems, sighs Adam to Eve
We need to re-invent our dreams...

## I Can Understand It All


Short and to the point, my head
Cracked open from the fall
I can understand it all
Often I have seen the waking
When the gay grave flowers sing
Man dreaming in the wide wind whirling
His works and progress out of hand
I can understand it all
But I've lost the calling
And the voice with which to call

Yet I can understand it all

## Breath and Dream

A leap
In the dark
You're on the bed
You lean
Your back
Against mine
It's nice
To have a body
To sleep with
The night
Sighs
The serpent
In the ear
Breath and dream
Conspire, repeat
It's nice
To have a body
To sleep with
Even a dog
Like you
With fleas

## Desert Rust

Desert rust. The heat
Letters from the heart
Spread out, texture
Out of context. Ruderal
Goo. Intimacies of light
Snapshots. Epiphanies
These stars, perhaps dead now
O indecent closure
Movement. Serpentine marks
Returning to the feral darkness
This undertow of blood as ancient
As sand, as Cherubims guarding Eden
The flaming sword turns
The dream waves undulating
The mind, the breath, nigrescent music
Silence and the music of silence
Our daily, broken rose...

## Stone

Under the map
Of the world
Where I sleep
Keeping time
By the heart
Worn on the sleeve
Worn to the bone
With loneliness
I dream
I am a stone
Skipping on the map's
Lapis lazuli
O dream waters
Dream azure
The shadow
Heart-shaped
Disappears
I plumb the dark
And secret deep
I ricochet
From déjà vu
I wake in shock
The reaches
Of the sea
Are cruel

## Self-Portrait

Who can tell the young man
No longer recognized in the photo
Fell in with the tigers of wrath
Along the road of excess
And dreams now of moon
And shadow, truth and sorrow
Out of my sleep, even speaks
Yea, half-sings behind my words
His ancient, warring lovesong?
Perhaps, mirror
This wide-load Santa
In the narrows of his trade
His suit blood-red
And blackened by the fire
Leaping at his feet
Perhaps he has the gift of memory
The heartbreak, the silence
To choose that voice
His youth can resonate

## One Long Dream

Bitter
Butterfly
My heart
Love's battered
Acrobat
Does our long dream still
Set fire to the cocoon?
That center ring
With roses
Those wings
That brush
The moon

## The Way

Is father's house mindless something to do a few manage
Media machines the majority a dead end a moon-spun fate
Supermarket things out of the blue the truth our lives
                                                possession
By possessions all these goods cursed others look laugh look
                                                away
Angels sing poverty liberty society's hip shapes the way I see
                                                red
My poor suit free reality happy anarchy gypsy journey to
                                        crowded fire
Confront mystery honey eating lion lamb dreamers revelation
                                        revolution
Can we buy try sky spoiled with pie bloody hands in style
                                                violence
Of unreason night silence eternal perhaps yes I'll wait only
                                                live
Lonely spoils the house things worse better go out weather
                                        get my own
Set order my own kind friend after all humankind kindness
                                        kills best

## Feeding My Dogs


Feeding my dogs in the backyard
Of the strange, Jewish professor
Who teaches math with a deck of cards
And ah, the aftermath—salami comfort
With the underbite of truth: There's no shame
Daniel, when a Christian loses to a Jew
Whose wife knows what she wants, is Irish
And away in the van, in the vanguard
Of the Revolution, heavy into Women's Liberation
Yes, raising my mother consciousness by feeding
My dogs yummies after losing at rummy
I see, unlike me, they don't know how to beg
And have no respect for proverbial wisdom
They bite my hand; with love I tell myself
Through yelling, Don't be greedy like George Macready
Remember him...the movie actor...
That scar on his right cheek
Little Caesar, shepherd/husky, the younger, black one
Also with a scar, looks like a gangster in a tuxedo
Whereas Josh, shepherd/collie, whose black face and
tan body
I rescued from a police station
Trots into battle with beauty marks
During the day they ride with me, Caesar round my neck
Josh in my pocket, the Scarf and the Thief, but at night
They can't stay where I stay so they rough it
In the backyard of the strange, Jewish professor
In a redbarn doghouse behind a makeshift fence
Which Josh, getting longer and stronger
Will tumble down soon
Negating the present escape routes of Caesar
O Caesar, black Caesar, the Scarf, the Digger
Digs into night, wraps himself round the moon
That old bone in the sky, as Josh the Thief picks sleep
From a pocket of stars and dreams of Jericho

## Sparrows

Sparrows
On the barb wire
That other one
So slick and pretty
How he up and eases
Over the fence
A red sun
Emblazoned
On his dark night
Listen
The radio, the soul sounds
Again I'm learning the ropes
That ring our routines
We talk always of time
In this house of numbers
Uniform, arm bands, rules
See the machine in the clinic
With timer, brake
And the ominous sentence
RELEASE WHEN HEAD STOPS
Where are the women?
Give us a glimpse. Something
Let their offensive body odors
Through the holes in the fences
My nose is open, waiting
Wanting the smell of women
And the women
What are they doing?
Are they obeying the rules?
It shall be permissible
For the women to roll
Their trousers up to a point
Not to exceed halfway between
Their ankle and their knee
Under no circumstances
Shall they be rolled
Up to the knee or above the knee
Yes, O Lord, spare us

Lead us not into
But deliver us from
Our dreams. Bless us
Keep the faithful
Count each sparrow
Our eyes turn toward
Each hair turning grey
On this, my almost
Forty-second birthday

## One More Graffito

Pity anyone
Who has to shit in nasty
Filthy Cleveland cockroach dead air
Evil shadow bars yellow dog cell
Meaty graffiti Uncle Sam junkie
Punk funk old mushroom clouded
Soupbone cough coffee
Cold monkey ass sand-
Wich is the way it is
City jail where
Taking my eyes off
The contemptible
Unkempt floor
I leave the future
Occupant of my cell
One more graffito
May your dirty dreams
Keep you sane

## A Prisoner of Dreams

Thick as my father
Though my belly
Is developing its own
Personality
May I make this
Nocturnal admission
I'm alive again
In the solitude
Of familiar living rooms
Lights out
In the mother dark I go
Till each asthmatic step
Puts my animal to bed
My head to dream
You out there
In the dark night
Of survival
Arrested and jailed
Bound over
Unable to make bail
Where you are
There's law and odor
Bad breath
And the slow elevator
Don't worry though
I'm coming
My word's my bond
I've promised you
The interview
You'll know me
I'm just like you
A prisoner of dreams
Our days
Cage us in
As the pen moves
In boredom
And in rage

## The Dogs of Morning

After the night
Has slipped away
Like a thief
With our dreams
After the voice
Has reached the suburbs
In the half-sleeping light
Are we ready, boys
To meet sweet Jesus?
Ready to be
At the beep and call
Of every indigent
And his mother
Wife, sister, girlfriend
Brother?
Caesar and Josh
Leap over me
Into the car
Like sailors
Drunk on liberty
We sail away to jail

## The Rain Poet

Save
My poems
For rainy
Days. Say
Them out
Loud. Listen
The rain
Applauds...

## Hail to the Chief

Hail to the Chief
Grief thief
George the Younger
The Florida-count wonder
The oil warmonger
With a strike-first thirst
Look! His rockets' red glare
Our pockets threadbare
The bombs bursting in air
O where's Osama's lair?
Does Dubya really care?
Listen...his nightmare prayer
O Daddy in Heaven
Like my birth daddy on earth
Let me attack Iraq
Let me bomb Saddam
Let America hear 43$^{rd}$ psalm
The Warlord's thy shepherd
Thou shalt not want
Thy civil liberties upfront
The Constitution is only
An old scroll of parchment
When the thunder rolls
That dog won't hunt
Tear it up
And repeat after me
My country 'tis of thee
Sweet Homeland Security
To thee I sing
To thy FBI
And if they're busy, try
Thy CIA, OK?
Cause now we all be hip
Listening to loose lips
Hungering for the Apocalypse
And to those rainy-day prophets
Who say again
What does it profit

A nation to gain
The whole world
And lose its own soul, I say
Which side are you on, boys?
Which side are you on?
Suicide or genocide?
Come on, boys, you gotta decide
Come on, boys, let's roll
Tear it up, 2, 3, 4
Hup, 2, 3, 4
Hup, 2, 3, 4
Tear it up...
Tear it up...
Tear it up...

## Again

Again you're returning
To the haunts of the lonely
The broken, on the childhood
Side of town. Read the signs
IGNORE ALIEN ORDERS. ROAD NARROWS
Till another deserves one good turn
Forgetting nothing, exit on the off chance
You may leap from your car in ecstasy
Hunger after light, divine for water
Turning over the heart's new leaf
To the dark music inside
Night coming on quickly, listen
If you were homeless, you'd be home now

**33**

Wet with terror in the green ghost rain
I clear my throat of the hopped-up frog
Clip a feather from my wounded wing
And fill the forest with my hardshell coo
Once, easy as pie between the sheets
I'd slip into my incestuous home
Take my room as bored as the rest
And wag my tongue when they'd throw a bone
Or incognito with a nom de plume
I'd hitchhike rides from hither to yon
Gospel and gossip I'd spread in bed
Charmed by the clime of the ivory moon
Or join King's men around the wall
Or scoot as a gadfly back to school
Or stay with friends, walk the dog
And talk at street corners to scorning men
And so I come to thirty-three
And find myself in this crucial fix
My bag of tricks upon a stick
Is as barren as the mule
As fruitless as the cursed tree
And even my old hobo shoes
Bring no new news to me...

## Rain

In the cold stillness
Of my car that will not start
I wait listening to the weather
Watching the white light of a street lamp
Spread its web on the grey window
Of that one, fixed on the windshield
A desperate moon caught in a season of tears
                    Traffic moves on
            A whirl of rubber on wet pavement
    A hum of engines—a hum that sounds like home
            To this one, waiting while it rains
                In a life that will not start

## Three Tears for Koizumi

Opposite me
Her beauty
Autumns forth
Now I see
The tears
That are not
There

My lips
Ribbons
In her hair
My tears
Her rainbow

It is cold
In New York
Shizue
Save for
The tears

## A Fool's Gold
*for Sid*


Cool in the kingdom of paradox
He treads an endless sea of blues
Frugal Argonaut
Found fleecing his own echo from the deep
As underground, in paying the rites-of-passage dues
His mouth of gold coins rude myths out of sleep
His hands are hard as no mere seaman's. Look!
A secret poet moonlighting on his black machine
His lust and wanderlust into a book
To lure each shopworn heart and clean
Deceivers and deceit away; those who mocked his quest
These latter catch his blackest pitch
Plain language as alive as death

## An Old Married Couple

I wish I were
An old married couple
Whose lives could flow
Like a stream of light
I'd lay my selves in bed
We'd talk, drink, read
Belch, fart, wheeze
Our dog nuzzled between us
We'd get up when we felt like it
Do whatever
Dance in our underwear
Throw a ball in the park
Praise the trees
Our hearts secure in the seasons
Dayshine to stars-end
A love feast
Tenable flesh, articulate bone

## Gonzales

Long past the bedtime of the wise
Past asphalt light, bright as tarnished gold
Under a fogbound moon, Gonzales & I go
To our secret place; there, crickets & stars & witches bloom
With room enough for him to run. What fun to watch that black dog move
Across the long green gulf of grass—lean against the wind
While I attend the shaggy end of things (thistles & burrs, weeds
Leaves, logs & broken limbs) chanting & whistling a hymn to him
Go, Gonzales, go
Chase those ghosts
With your black magic
Ghosts from a grandfather time
They have waited all these years to play

— 57 —

## The Heart of It All

Ohio
I'm following you
Down the road
I'm tailgating you
I'm so close I can read
Your license plate
It says you're the heart of it all
But it seems your heart has turned
Arctic cold
With six months of darkness
Six months of light
Who can make it through?
When a half-year of days
Is one long, cold, black night
Who can survive to praise the light?
All is grey now; the sky
Is filled with waves of gulls
The airwaves with violins
Into the Flats we go
Down to the river
O throw your heart
Into its fire, Ohio
Let it melt
I'll be your tug
And pull you
To the sea...

## Words

Those in power always want
Those in poverty to live on poetry
The best things in life are free
They're fond of saying. Of course
If you help yourself to what's
Second best, they lock you up
And if you tell them all you wanted
Was just a little bit more on your plate
They'll hit you with, Man shall not live
By bread alone. They certainly don't
They've got the bread and the gravy
The meat and potatoes, the Army
The Air Force, the Marines and the Navy
And what have we got? Our loneliness
And our need to break bread
For that sound breaks the silence between us
And out of that broken silence tumbles everything
A cornucopia of words to feed the heart
Night words that arise and fall with each breath
Each shadow, words as light as light
Whose wings brush against us
And we are never the same
Words that are famous
With only four letters
Like food, love, home, sing...

## School of Night

Moon-
Light like
A stone
Falls on
The water
Bone-white
Breaking into
The laughter
Of fish
Of what
School
Are you
Heart?
A lily pad
Floating
On the sleeve
Or caught
A frog
In the throat
Wanting only
To croak...

## Local Color

Behold
The noble savages
How charming
They bare their teeth
In freeloading hostility
How crooked
Like the river
Is their pork
Barrel politics
As they slaughter
The hog
In Cuyahoga again
And again
The children
Of the crime
Of poverty
Children of the stars
Of the night
And the city
Witness as victims
This feeding frenzy
Drown in its gaudy
River of blood

Even the god
Of the plagues
In Egypt
Demanded only
The first-born

## Warning of Danger

In the fields
In the evening
The cows
Those bathers
At the beach
Possess such
A nonchalance
I would leap
Out of envy
From the highway
Into their green
Waves of earth
Were it not
For this low-
Flying bird
Crossing the car's path
Like some bad-
Luck black cat
This morning
Standing at the window
I saw a real cat move
The Cary Grant of
*To Catch a Thief*
Not on buildings
But the leafy
Branches of a tree
Three, four stories high
If the cat falls
I thought aloud
We both die

Thought aloud
Against the crow's
Hammering wings
And awful
Caw-caw-caw
Warning of danger

## Poetry Fool

No fool
For poetry
Save me
Rose and read
To rows of the living
Rows of the dead
Then fled
Sped away
Ran the red-
Lights home
Where dogbreath kisses
And whistling kettle
Finally settled me
Down in the yellow
Kitchen chair
There to consider
The heart's dark
Questions like
Why am I still
Here and there
While everywhere
Fugitive, soldier
Refugee feet
Go left, go right
Repeat, repeat
Despite what
All the poetry fools
Of the school of night
May write, left, right
Anguish is still
The world's official
Language...
O save us
Stillness
Turning into light
Awakening the birds
Shaping the air
With song, these words

This little green prayer
This ancient
Longing to belong

## The Horde's Prayer

Our Vaterland
Whose Art is Super, Man
Hallowed be Thy Bomb
Thy King Kong come
Thy Dung ding-dong
From Washington to Saddam
Give us this Day our daily Dread
Our daily Dead
And forgive us our Exploits
As we give forth to Those who exploit us
And lead us not into the Hot
But deliver us first from feeling Evil
For Thine is the Freedom and the Pow
And the Old Glory Wow
Wherever there's ever
A Menace

# The Adventures of a Wild-Eyed Western Boy

Once upon a down and out
When time meant more than money
And I was as spoiled as the sky was pie
I heard the sun went West and died
And curious to see what killed the cat
I followed suit, suitcase in hand
Threw a cautious thumb to the wind
And whispered darkly, I'm a mad madcap
I wandered as low as a grasshopper's knee
And when first I turned to leaves of grass
I kissed Mississippi: the cracker smacked back
O black democratic soul en masse
The papers called it a Freedom Ride
I forget the Alamo in San Antone
But not Mrs. Gomez in Crystal City
Her lingo was Spanish and the gringo's spinach
Was moved to the beat of the sun on her back
She kept the noise happy in flypaper rooms
And all eyes popped when her green-aged daughter
Barefoot lovely, ran for water...
Near Indio I met a blue Indian who
Must have been bad: only the dead are good
He had firewater secrets, a fire in the desert
And tears in the chapel as above the altar
Rose an Indian Jesus on a cloud of peyote
On the red hue of angels, on the howl of coyote
While outside circled the white bird of prey
Noble and savage...just like the good old days
So this is it and here I am
I said to myself as I hit San Fran
In the promised land of the promised land
To the welcome committee I yelled, Hello
Nobody answered, so I lay low
And broke the silence with bread and wine
And a song I had made
Just to pass the time rhyming

*Here lives a race in pursuit of youth*
*Violence its beauty, comfort its truth*
*And goodness knows where it has gone*
*Off to a war I know is wrong*
*So my name is shame, but I'm not to blame*
*And I'm sure you're feelin' just the same*
*But if you're really feelin' blue*
*Don't do yourself violence; I'll comfort you*
*'Cause I'm a wild-eyed Western boy*
*My trade's good lovin' and my trademark's joy*

## The Tears of Jesus

After the mayoral
Sweep of the homeless
From the streets into jail
Jesus wept
The mayor then ordered
The tears to be swept away, too
The tears of Jesus are bad for business
During the Christmas rush
I mean, come on, said the mayor to Jesus
Don't be such a big baby

## Dark Rider

I've crossed this country
Uneasy with fools
And stopped at missions
For the soupbone of truth
Singing
Nowhere to go
Let's go there again
Nothing to do
Let's do it

        I've left a trail
        Of breadcrumb words
        For the alphabet birds
        That follow me
        Singing
        O dark rider
        On an endless road
        In this season of shadow
        There's blood on the wind

                Now a mad arrow strikes
                The fragile banquet begins
                The fugitive heart
                Finds its sadness again
                Singing
                Ha HaHa
                Da DaDa Da Da
                TraLa LaLaLa
                La La

## Homeless Prayer

How soft the sidewalk
On a cold, spring night
How dry the spring
Not a fountain for our thirst
Only day-old for our appetite
Our chums, the seagulls, come
To share a few bagel crumbs
O let us pray for the brutes
Who are dumb. Let us pray
For the brutes who are dumb

## If I Had Wings

If I had wings
I'd fly after nightfall
To the heart of the city
To the darkest part of poverty
There—out in the open under bright lights
Those steamy places where the homeless sleep
Night after night. If I had wings, ribs, pizza
Donuts, bagels, pastries and simply water
I'd get it together, whatever the weather
If I had wings, I'd spread them out along
With these other things against the night hunger
For a feast in the belly of the beast
If I had wings, this would be
My latitude, longitude
Altitude and attitude
If I had wings...

## Comeback City

The hue and cry
Fanatics make
On downtown streets
At night
After the homeys
Again win
A big one
At the Jake
Keep the homeless
Who sleep on sidewalks
Awake
Come back, City
Give these forgotten
Princes of the street
Something sweet
Before they sleep
And answer me
This big one
When will you love
Your foolish
School-children
As much as you love
Your millionaires?

## Ohio Rhetoric

Nobody who says
This country is great
Sleeps on a grate
We're here
'Cause we've been there
In the dead heat
In the dead, beat cities
In God we rust
On the heartland express
To nowhere
We are Cleveland
Cincinnati, Chillicothe
Akron, Canton, Dayton
Toledo, Youngstown
Columbus, Springfield
Steubenville, Circleville
Alliance, Defiance...
That's the ticket
That's what we're building
An alliance
To show our defiance
To tell the Pentagon
Enough is enough
Be gone
You're the biggest
Con game in town
To tell the White House
The homeless are coming
To move in
Into the attic
Into the basement
Into the Rose Garden
Into Air Force One
Into Camp David
Into the Metro—
Trains would make
Nice mobile homes

To tell Congress
Yes
Affordable housing
For the poor
But don't forget
The rich and the super-rich
The influence
Of their affluence
The money they make
Out of our misery
They need housing, too
Shuffle them off
To the big house
And the workhouse
You don't have
To be Sherlock
To figure this out
Homeless need homes
Before stadiums need domes
And HUD rhymes with THUD
And that's the other shoe dropping
Are you listening, America?
Not all the homeless
Are on the street
There are invisible homeless
Those who feel
A homelessness in the heart
The ones who wonder, America
Where your heart is
Whether you're still home
Land of the free
Home of the brave
What does that mean?
A free ride for the rich
And the poor are free
To land in the street
The new home of the brave
The street is hard
And millions are just
A paycheck away

And millions must pay
An unconscionable percent
Of their income on rent
Turn your back
On the homeless
And nearly homeless
You turn your back
On your own
Turn your back
On your own
Watch out!
You turn your back
On the future
America, it's time
To behave, to be brave
To save yourself
And house the homeless now
If you don't, you're just
A BIG FAT CASH COW
Ready for the slaughter
By your sons and daughters
Who are not alone
Looking for a home

## Dark Rider Sings Again

O dark rider
On an endless road
Thick as thieves
With the wind
And your shadow
You cross this country
Uneasy with fools
And stop at missions
For the soupbone of truth
Vagabond bondsman
Fired up in jail
Raising hell
Then bail for the devil
You leave a trail
Of breadcrumb tears
For the alphabet birds
That follow you
Is it death or a woman
Calling you home
Come quick as a jackknife
To the mumblety-peg ground
And Sing
Ha HaHa
Da DaDa Da Da
TraLa LaLaLa
La La

## Quarterback

Fetal fatal, fiddle-faddle
Baby plays with Death's rattle in the womb
Hurry-scurry, helter-skelter
Even odds there is no shelter from the doom
The wind'll blow dust
The iron will rust
The worms'll crawl through the skull
O what can we break when there is no bread?
And how can we breathe when they have us by the throat?
Now don't close your eyes
And tell me that you're blind
No
Let the lies
Die behind the lids
The heart in the holster hangs the man
Soft keyhole on the shoulders
Now I move
My bloodhound senses quarterback the wind...

# Countdown

Desperate at the pin-dropped quiet
Of our quick sand in the glass
We are the lost, the transient losers
Hurricaned in the eye of the haystack needle
Riffraffed and rabble-roused and, honey eating, riddled
We are Jacob and Adam sweating in exile
And the blood donor at the rock, cupped in human sleep
It's time now: time to take the tribal trip
Past the cast of hawks, some soft morning
From the weeping pillow leap, the almanac sun
Whistling in on a host of sparrows as numbered
And remembered as the hairs
The fingertipped shadow in the hollow of the thigh
And new names wrestled from the crippling dawn
It's time: time to go the primal step
Over the labor of moles
Mountainward to the beat of the bush,
the flameshaped tongue
Slips off our shoes and weaves us into a mosaic net
As talisman against moth, rust, and thieves
And a roughcoat against the wind
The bestial mystery grieving in the heart
Begin the burning journey home
The hour is come
Time's sleight of hand gives Death his due at leisure

## Sailor on the Road
*for my sister*


I believe
I'm beginning to be bored
I chuckle to myself
Remembering the dowager
Who delivered this line
With deadpan panache
At a party in Key West
One balmy evening
In the late sixties
Now
The last straw
Of the scarecrow's blown away
The ground's as white as a sheet
In the bone-chilling cold
And smoky breath of the Midwest
I crack my knuckles
Avoid chuckholes
Whistle
Shimmy with the car
And sing
The yellow submarine
VW I drive
Is hell below zero
Fire and ice
Nor is there
Comfort from heaven
Save the moon
Breaking through
Reveling in its light
As thought after thought
Reveals
In the headlights
The broken, white line
Guiding the mind's eye
This is the white zone
I am alone

With Christmas spirit night sauce Cadillac fish noise
Hot lead-footed mouse house fly paper hat slave
Wood blood cell magic whale book
Snakeroot ant tie matter out fox leather glove print
Horse feather eye wash mulberry pepper squall
Mahogany coal cap flag-tailed deer lie
Lightning man's burden birch perch frost bait
Water Russian metal plague gasoline wall cloud
Oak-throated sparrow power meat heat elephant irrelevant
White thoughts from the broken, white line
On the highway to Kay
As her brother
I've an open invitation
To the chaos of her life
And know the map
Between here and Chi
Like the back of my hand
Each blue path, scar and blade of hair
Traffic is light, the road clear
Nothing has happened to slow me down
No acts of God so far
No dying horses' blood on the windshield
No flooding of hope
No auto-fellatio at James Dean Plaza
Nor Hoosier sweetheart's quicksand shoulder
I have not been pulled over
By the voice of reason
If my luck holds
I knock on wood
With my fingers crossed
I should make good time
Zoom through the boondocks
Arrive at the backdoor
If it's open
I'll be sitting pretty soon
On Kay's sofa
A bellyful of road
And eyes glazed
I believe
I'm getting my second wind

The mills have turned
The night sky red
Delighting sailors
On ore boats as well
As steel millionaires
Breathing hard in mansions
Trying to think
Of new ways to steal
Listen, mates
I'm a sailor on the road
And have been since that afternoon
The Old Man found me
Pen in hand, lost in thought
Off duty in the galley
The captain smiled as he entered
What are you doing, son, he asked
Keeping track of your earnings?
No, sir, I said, I'm writing poetry
Dead silence
His face turned red
Then he exploded
There ain't no poetry on a steamboat
Aye, aye, Captain Bligh, I thought
That was enough poetry for me
I put away my Sinbad verse
Any freshwater salt could've read
The handwriting on the bulkhead
When we made port
I hit the bricks quick
Eighty-sixed, bag and bagatelle
Thankful I hadn't been deep-sixed
In a wavy grave
Ah, Roastaroma Mocha Spice
I'm just your average teahead
I whirl my silver spoon
While on the airwaves
Early jazz
Older than I am
As old as the King of Siam
And all his Milky Way of cats
Nine-lived in silk pajamas

O star-winged
Hawk-light
Dark home
Trees
This open door
Welcome
Is perfect

## Roldo

True
Gray, slanted rain may
Wake or lull to sleep
The just and the unjust
Yet
Does rain forget it's rain
When it mingles
With our sorrow?
Now
Who's that in the wind
And rain, raking muck
Shaking out the truth?

## Even the Broken Letters of the Heart Spell Earth

Even the broken letters of the heart
Spell...Earth. Let the heart beat for the trees
Their perfection, the ancient rain, the open spaces
Along the river, the species that are endangered
The tiger burning bright, the flower, the honey bee
The frozen places of silence, the cruel bottom
Of the sea, the schools of fish made truant
And in the sky the ozone's wound and the bird's nest
And the eye that rests on the sparrow...

Even the earth of the brokenhearted can heal

## In the Nick

In the nick of time and place
Blood from the rainbow flows
Our earth, so rooted in that red
With ready violence waits

Consumed by rage
Or vagrant with a tune
I lay my head, misshapen
On the white breast of the moon

# Fruits and Vegetables

It's raining, I'm on the West Side to get my thumb X-rayed. Was it Lutheran
Where Uncle Art died? I cut through the Market, through decades of fruits
And vegetables to World War II. There I am again with Sis on the way to school
In this same arcade, where everything's alive and tells a story
Like poor, young Sweet Potato, after telling Cherry Tomato they cantaloupe
'Cause he's squeezed dry making payments on that lemon they're driving
Goes out with the boys for a spinach, pulls up to the nearest pumpkin
You help us? We need asparagus. Beet it, cries a big grape, who looks like
He belongs in the zucchini see we're closed, and throws Corn out on his ear
I'd call that a cauliflower, Artichokes with emotion and swings open the car door
Avocado, desperado. The boys jump out swinging like Tarzan and the apricots
I don't wanna die-ah, says the Papaya, Call me a cabbage. I'm leaving. Too late
After the Rhubarb wires home to Lima for beans, the boys're bailed out of jail
And they sail off to work. But it's not up to parsley, so the eggplant's out
On strike. Pears of goons on celery stalk picket limes, peppering them with insults,
You dirty radishes, this is the last strawberry the hatchet or we'll squash you, we'll
Mango you, we'll string your beans up by the nectarines, we'll brussel your sprouts
Turnip tomorrow, you'll get more than the raspberry, you'll go home with a pineapple
Up your ask me no questions, I'll tell you no lying sweet talk, says Sweets
And pulls out a banana, splits open those sons of peaches, pits and all
He really creams them, so Broccoli surrenders to the Onion, love is everywhere

Sweet Potato grabs Tomato, Yam nuts about you, honeydew, lettuce tangerine
You can see I know my peas and cucumbers, and no unrhymed orange
Nor crazy plum could have made me hum that day happy as a watermelon
Only carrots, loud and hard as nails. What's in the bag, kid? Updoc
Bugs Bunny on the streetcar, I eat my roots, roll my eyes heavenward and salute
Now, lucky me, I'm two wars older, running late as usual
Where is everyone? O, it's Thursday, the Market's closed. Our friends
The fruits and vegetables are off today. The arcade's almost empty
There are only those crossing guards who wish to keep dry and these gentlemen
Who do not, the morning body count. Are you my lost uncle, my brother
Itinerant artist, veteran of the starvation army? Last night was it the slammer
Or a hallelujah flop? And you, old man, you know by heart those nameless dogs
Where your dead soldiers lie. Why are you so grave, soldiers? You've tailor-mades
I see. You've no port, no muscatel. Well, you've come together this day unsaved
A black-toothed crew—tattooed, blue, open flies, eyes of salt and humor, surviving
Wars and rumors. I catch images of myself, my breath in the bad air, hurry on…

## A Prisoner's Story

As I danced
They came for me
We danced around
They hauled me to court
Twelve good kangaroos and true
Naturally I was convicted
Contributing to the delinquency
Of a rainbow. The sentence?
Life in this prism
I hate bars, I yelled
The only smile they cracked
Was mine. Desperation set in
One of my multiple personalities
Escaped, secured my release
By then I'd lost face
No one recognized me
The grapevine buzzed
Like a bloody chainsaw
Vanished, thin air
Disappeared, not a trace
Abracadabra
Poof!
Now they call me
The Flamboyant Silence
And the younger ones
Pops, the old man of color

## There are Saints in the City
### *for Ralph Delaney*

There are saints in the city
Moving through the streets
Through sadness and shadow
No fiery chariot from the sky
Only an ordinary, beat-up station wagon
Earthbound, moving toward the fires
Along the picket line at Greyhound
Where the homeless joining hands with strikers
Keep warm, keep watch, keep it together
Till out of the ordinary
Not a miracle of doves bringing peace
But carte blanche comes love's daily bread
As light as the bird in the hand
These are the saints who use the pot
That didn't melt to make the soup
To take to the heart of the city
There at Public Square in the shadow of the Tower
Amid the rats, the abatements, the greed
They've weathered the cold, midnight air
Yes, there are saints in the city
Moving through sadness and shadow
Through the projects with crayons and food
Looking, listening for beauty
For the art of the people
For the poetry of the soul, fired up
Hungering in poverty for the light of justice
How ironic, Ralph
In *The Plain Dealer's* headline
You're labeled a social worker
How often they
Along with administrators
Police, public officials
Hold attitudes that epitomize
An insensitivity toward the poor
That dehumanized spirit
You sought to overcome

They also call you
A friend of the poor
But if everyday
You eat with the poor
Sleep with the poor, walk
And talk, breathe with the poor
You are the poor, friendly or not
Come out of your coma, Ralph
Speak to us. We know if you could
Your first words would forgive
Your enemies and those who beat you
You'd wish to teach them to fight
Like Gandhi and King
Ralph, this may not be the right time
But we confess...you often bore us
With your constant talk about the poor
In jail, on the street, in the projects
Where you work, where you live
But Ralph, come back, bore us again
And this time, forgive your friends

## From the Life of Anna Mae Stewart
*a WW II poem*


That little boy
Who looks like Mickey Rooney
And lives on the other side of the park
Tells me there are lovers in the bushes
In fact it's a local Frankie Sinatra
Heart throb named Mooney who's half the act
Suddenly love's four-letter thought—
Would Mooney find me beautiful
Invite me into his greenery
To see the new moon rising?
No jejune moon for our Frankie
War news whirling in his ear
He whispers, Them bastards. They won't ration our dreams...
Now at Merrick House where I work
This woman coming in seems to know the Thompson boy
I ask him, Is that your mother, Danny?
That's not my mother. My mother's beautiful, he says
O, will the war yield me a boy-turned-man
And boys of my own to praise my beauty?
And daughters with beauty to be praised?
Or will the world lose such fierce innocence
Among its fallen warriors?

# Two

## "And the Heart, Still Shining, Sings"

## Eye of Gold

Eye of gold
Lake of fire
The ghost-chanting tree
All images of the elements
Enrapture me
With their restless alchemy

How things spring forth
And summer up
Then fall to sleep
In winter down

Here is
The stone I found
Move it around
The ear of the hare
Is the beak of the bird
At the edge of the dinosaur

## Bearing the Burden

Bearing the burden
Into the wild, into the wild light
The burden of words into the wild
Light of the dead, of the dead stars
Nocturnal poet
Coming out of sleep on the sweet mare of dream
Moves beyond the eye and the piety of animals
Beyond lost artifice, Edisonian invention
Beyond the vehicular theft of silence
To the breath of the dance
To love's profound loneliness
O ancient moon, blood on the moon
Tree—leaf, branch and shadow
We are rooted in the earth's sorrow
We wait for the fall
The axe to fall, this poem

The shining edge of the blade

## This Quiet Night

This quiet night
And the murdering ant
An army on the sidewalk moves
Carrying its starlit prey
Across the chalked children's game

This wax moon night the rabbit runs
His white tail bobbing as he weaves
Through backyards to the black, black trees
Suddenly a voice, cat or child, troubles the silence

O down these streets where sleeping dogmas lie
Lo, the flickering lamplight moth shadowboxes with the wind
As my friend, the talker, talks: widening the hole in his shoe
Till all his words arrive on time
Bloodshot, in the gunsight of dawn

That quiet night the dark cargo of my heart
Pitched on the green grave wave and broke...

## Lines

*A Cleveland Poem*


i have a city to cover with lines
   d.a. levy
Love is a black-faced loon
   Seymour Lieberman

The thrill is gone
What's next?
   Peg Swiniarski

Forget the poetry
Poetry has ruined my life
   Tim Joyce

Trees are perfect
   Geoff Singer

The person who said
One nuclear bomb
Can ruin your whole day
Didn't know what kind of day I had
   Tom Schwendeman

I'm losing money just talking to you
   Buzzy Linhart

Poetry is theft
   Daniel Tompson

## Jazz

Too many novelty acts
News from mutants
Echoing on the walls
Of the nuclear cave
The new wavers rave
Then somewhere
You hear
Jazz
And you say to yourself
This is _real_ music
And soon
You're two bites
Out of the apple
Eve and Adam
Moving slowly, subtlety
As the serpent moves
Through the black, fallen leaves of Eden

## To Sleep and Forget

To sleep and forget
The evening sky
The promises of the city
I lie, fallen roses
Round my bed
White flowers drawn
From my sick breath
By hand, though
No sleight of hand
Can take away the pain
Take heart, I say
And the heart is taken
Its sleight of breath
Extends the poetry of flesh
Returns love to the earth
Where the hand
Again dreaming
Writes in the dust

## Song

Earthquake questions after midnight
Turn into a morning song
Radio and going nowhere
How I love to move along
Light is there to help each body
Sing the sorrow Jesus saves
Open all the wounds to healing
Call us dancing from our graves

O the catch-a-death hard weather
O the struggle without end
Now the streets have no faces

Now silence is our friend

## The Trip

Wide spots
Through an open grave
That windfall of nature's trivia
Huff and puff of semi-crazed
Monsters raising a hurricane field
Reading, riding and the arithmetic
Of road maps: match what you can
From signposts in numerology
Mixed as always with the language
Of the land, like EAT FOOD EXIT GAS
And all that other ad verse et cetera
Upsetting the vision of the wild horses
We race on
The broken white line, the hopscotch yellow
The endless string of unbiblical crosses
Where feathered sentinels, our voices in their claws
Sit in silent watch above the mounting death
Above the nameless carrion once wild and tame
And now the lights of the West turn on
As the sun slips off in perspective
And the lovers lurch toward the heart of the dark

# The Blood of the Artichoke
*for Kevin Williams*


Last call for art at the Artichoke
One more song from the band
One last poem from the poet
After that, performance art
We cut Kevin's throat
And give our regards to old Broadway
To chrome moonlight, to steel-mill air
To shadow men behind the neon
Face east...Hubcap heaven
West...Kevin's final resting place
Grass, a tree, a rusty fence and gate
And flowers sent out of loneliness
By the cool-hand hustlers of Memories
The grim pilgrims of Happy Hour
That old-timer, cane in hand
Coming out of the Hub Café
Where only customers are allowed in the can
Beats on the sidewalk a last tattoo
O for a bugle boy from Broadway School
And a fast Buck Bros. lay-a-way plan
Cross the street to the vacant lot
Read the wall...Mail Pouch...Pure leaf
No Drugs to Chew...No Stems to Smoke
There, against the hard mouth's appetite
The season's dark, the broken stars in flight
Write Kevin his epitaph
At the Heart of Art
Is the Blood of the Artichoke

## The Poet in White Tails

The poet in white tails
Standing on the overturned
Dump truck, used as a wall
In the carnivorous junkyard
Throws caution to the four winds
Reads, then releases his poems...
They sail from his hand on white paper
Doves against the threatening sky

## Soldier

Down the alley of affluence
Round the corner of despair
Or anywhere abandoned things are grown
I seek my treasure in that trash

A smashed muffler one night
Scraped my heel & begged me take him home
Now, cleaned & dry, he guards my fire
Forgetting he once coughed pollution
Fell off the wagon & ended up almost a guttersnipe

So there he stands, my scrappy soldier
No hunk of junk for the autocrat's habit
But shaped in battle with Goodyear et al
He's now a warrior, a work of art
A gift, perhaps, of prophecy

## Night Vision

She wants me to go along; it's a long way
How's your night vision?  she asks
We leave in the evening; I get behind the wheel
It's not that I drive fast...I change lanes constantly
Go on the sidewalk, go through every redlight I can
We hit downtown. She says, I think I can take it from here
I need a ride home; I see you. What's the story? you say
It's not that I drive fast, I answer, It's my night vision
I can see things you wouldn't believe. You drive me home
On one condition...Keep your damn eyes closed all the way
Before we get there, I cheat. Watch out for the giraffe, I yell
Too late, not for the giraffe, in fact he's still wearing
                                    that blue hat
But his piano is a total wreck

## Love's Anthology

She came to me
With gathered flowers
Her Love's anthology
Each verse she petaled
Round my heart
A chain to set me free
But troubled
By the double dark
Of lateness
Of death
I broke the chain
My heart and hers
Then couldn't
Catch my breath
The flowers fell
Each syllable
An echo of a tear
Till she whispered
Don't despair
Breathe through eye
Through ear
From blood dreams
To hand's artifice
Love rides
The sensuous air

## Beauty and the Bird

Out of loneliness
I have fashioned
A bird that does not sing
Save when rare occasions bring
Stark beauty
Then bird and I are one and we
Go mad with song and beat our wings
And through imagination's eye
We even fancy we can fly
Beyond the skin of things
Then earth's
Sad face comes round again
Reminds us of the cage we're in
And how stark raving mad we've been
To think we're saved by beauty

## Diner Poem
*for Jerry's*


The sky is red
The sky is a mirror
Over the bleeding, dying city
But we are alive
In a once-in-a-blue-moon mood
Ready to move
And that's the crime
Sue Blue, down on her luck in L.A.
Living close to the bone
And the nerves' ganglia
Once she and her son, Navarro
Lived for months in their car
Told me during a visit
With her breathless mother
Daniel, if I had to live in
Cleveland, I'd become a criminal
Tonight, the moon is blue
Anarchy's in the air
It's a crime to breathe
There's an all-points bulletin
On all moonlight conspirators
I drive the getaway car
We're riding the crest of a crime wave
A wave of emotion, crimes of the heart
Crimes of passion in the night season
But you, you're as cool as roses
There in the suicide seat
As we speed out of the desperate city
Past sweet, suburban dreams and ennui
You're a fast-talking, wisecracking
Chain-smoking Bette Davis
A High Sierra Ida Lupino
A Dead Reckoning crazy blonde
No one dare call crazy, Liz Scott
Ready to bail out of Bogie's pocket
With a kiss and a smoking gun

What fun. Geronimo, Let's go
271 to 14 to 43 to the city of 4 deaths
To the city of intense poetry, Kent
We'll stop at Jerry's Diner
You can have anything you desire
I go for the home fries
And to hang poetry flyers
There's usually a poet hanging out
I believe they keep one in residence
To amuse the tourists
And welcome the returning alumni
Sometimes it's a bard
With a yard of animal poems
Full of all their sounds
Or the waitrons, the cooks
They're the secret poets
Poets of the spud
And you're in the poem
They're in your poem
I know. If it's not too late
We'll call and ask Jake what's shakin'
Roman might be in town
Maybe Major made a wager
And is back from the track with the jack
I once asked Maj
Whether he was born in the year of the horse
Of course I'll always play the straight man
For the one who can do the Camptown races
With Buddha and has a voice like Lowell Thomas
I'm an Irishman, not a Chinaman, he told me
I was born in the year of the potato
Some say potato, some say potahto
Some say mares eat oats, some say
That's a horse of a different color
That shouldn't be changed in midstream
That things are in the saddle and ride mankind
Though Gable said in *Boom Town*
(1940—the year Maj was born)
Great day for the race. What race? The human race
And who are the winners after all?

Conquest, War, Famine, Death
Ah, we're here at last in the homestretch
On our journey to the end of the night
What? The lights are dim
The door is locked. The diner is closed
Again the question is now
Where do we take our loneliness?
Jerry's is closed. An era is dead
But we are alive
And I drive the getaway car
The moon is blue
Anarchy's in the air
You're as cool as roses
And ready to move
Geronimo. Let's go

## C Street

Driven into the street
By what?  Inexorable grief
The moon of hunger
Boredom, my dog...
This life on the high wire
Life in midair, life fallen
Between the cracks into the heartless dark
Blindly I tap, tap, tap
Like some desperate telegrapher
A message to the world
I want light
I want a shining path
I want flowers of illumination
I want lightning and thunder
I want a cornucopia of light
I want a clean, well-lighted place
I want a wall of light
Where the cool meet the hot
Where the underground
Rubs shoulders with the underworld
I want neon Trotsky
I want C Street to be alive with light
I want the cornbeef conspirators to lighten up
I want the wall of light to be a wall of art
Where the hipsters and the tipsters
And the junkies for all seasons wail and reason
Those with a Dow Jones jones
Those with a nose for news, reading the Times
Those poets of the night, versed in survival and crime
Those who joke and smoke cigars
While under the stars their cars are ticketed
Listen to the heartbreak now
To the ticker-tape tales of emotional meltdown
Of lives turned into chopped liver
To beef after beef, to a knock worse than death
To the baloney of the lonely
Were the years with Irv the wilderness?
Will C Street lead to the promised land?

Ask Sheldon. Ask Dianne
Ask the weekend bar-trekkers pumped up on twilight
ozone
Ask the old-timers: Ben, Harry, Sid, Seymour, Jerry
Go deep. Go below the ego. Go sub Irv
And say to the id, Here's looking at you, kid
It's not hunger or boredom but loneliness
That makes each face a mirror...

## Tell Chief Wahoo

Tell Chief Wahoo
Wounded Knee
Crazy Horse
Sand Creek
Sitting Bull
Little Big Horn
Whisper in his ear
The trail of tears
Tecumseh
Cochise
Joseph
John O'Mic
Geronimo
Let him know
When this false face
Red Sambo
With its Uncle Tomahawk grin
And Pinocchio lie of a nose
Goes
He shall rise up
On the wings of eagles
Dance to the drumming
And dream
Not what the White Man
Deems important
The pennant race
At Fort Jacobs
But the human race
The wilderness
Of his own imagination
His original face...

## Kentucky Luck

After the race
A scavenger darkness
Blackbird picking
At the blackened fur
At the hare's foot
Luck times four
Flatter than
The floogee
With the floy floy
Let me balance this
With the day's loss
Pay my respects
To life, to death
And give my heart's
Breath to the green wood
The fallen rock
The roadwork ahead

## Love in the Arcade

Weightless
Love's astronaut
I float in the Arcade
Past the bridge's
Sundry ghosts and time
Tiers of time
Tiers of iron
Cast and wrought
Past brass
Past balcony
Gryphon and star-
Striped banner
O arpeggios of steel
Toward the light
In your eyes, toward
The heart's breath
Inside our Arcadia
Where your hands wait
Like a bird among branches
A hidden dream
An enclave on fire
Desire encircled by beauty
Beauty encircled by desire
As the tree makes wood
In silence, these words
Disappear into a kiss...

# Numbers

I never get laid
Just a stinky finger
Last Saturday I rolled
All night on the floor with a psychic
A numerologist; she did a chart on me
Liked me 'cause of my wonderful numbers
I had met her on the telephone
I'm into numbers, she says
Well, I say, I live in the ghetto
But I never play; I'm beyond
Numbers: I'm into Deuteronomy
Joshua, that's one of my dogs, and
Judges: I get people out of jail; the
Judges set bail, so I'm friendly
With those black-robed rascals
She was friendly, too, invited me over
I moved fast but didn't continue
Down my biblical path, didn't tell her
I'd lost touch with Ruth, have been
Ruthless ever since. Instead
I began to speak of love, to count its ways
But she was numb to love, or rather
Loved only numbers, had mine
And led me to believe they'd never add up
And I'd be out considering the agony
Of the roses, out of luck and balance
Spinning by moonlight toward the pitiless dawn

## Claudia of the Cats

Wishing for fish
Fowl or a whole mouse
From a mousehole
Gives cat that
Beyond the Mona Lisa
But not quite Cheshire
Look. It's the Golden Gate
Our alchemical cat
Stretching from Colette
To the purple Buddha
That's from Colorado, says Claudia
Who's all the way from Germany
Where she once killed a cow
Now, home before her daughter's
Dark laughter, with only time to kill
She delights in the winter light
An illicit pipe, Charles Aznavour
In this quiet zone
The office disappears
A spider works its silver thread
No one shoots the piano player
With her blue, peace-symbol tattoo
She had marched over there
Mad as a March hare
Turned from prayer and hurled
Stink bombs at the U.S. Embassy
(Olfactory workers of the world, unite)
Right to the heart of the target
A penchant for violent heroes
She zeroes in, thumbs her nose
At our machismo, yet
Lets me off the hook, hooked as I am
On her Marx Brothers kittens
Who turn my love-is-blind eyes red
And take my breath away

# Car Talk

No kisses
While driving
I told her
Keep your lips
On the road

Night is a poem
She whispered
Whose quiet falls
Like a pin
From the weight
Of dancing angels

Pain, I said
Fancy cane and all
Permits me
This poem noir
This silent dance

Death's sister, she said
The Angel of Sleep
Vanishes into a cloud of mirrors
A pillow with a silver lining
O Cocteau, cockatoo, cock-a-doodle-do

There's movement, I said, strokes
The color of ghosts, descending
The staircase from heaven
To grow bones, to dress up in nudity
And once upon the down of earth, to rest

Then lips are wings, she cried, the
Word shapes the mouth. Breath is
Blood and feather

We're almost
There, I said

## And the Black Pie Company, too

Sittin' on a stoop
Outside the Yellow Chicken Co-op Coop
Just a hop from the Gutenberg Machine Shop
And the Black Pie Company, too
She was lovelier than the sun
And I was sure blondes have more funny
Ways to make me wanna say, Hey! Hey! Hey!
But you know she knew I wouldn't stay
And that I never write, that is, I'm not a man of letters
Though I try so hard to imitate my betters
Like stampin' things & stringin' clever feathers in my cap
And I like to meet the girls & boy!
Snap my fingers & be happy on the map
Then she said before I kissed her
Listen, mister, you beware the Butterfly
He stuttered he may try to b-b-bell the Cat
He wants you dressed as Judas Goat but smellin like a rat
Well, I was glad to help her carry groceries to her pad
And use her double mattress as my hideaway
Though we knew the troubled Butterfly
Would flutter by someday & I would be a rat & go away
And leave her sittin' lovelier, sunnin' on the stoop
Just a hop from the Shop
And the Black Pie Company, too

## In the Dark

Somewhere in the darkened theater
There's a woman who will break your heart
Does she read Pauline Kael?
Does the wind that carries the gold dust away
Carry her laughter? Does she like
Her popcorn plain? Just like you
She slouches down to watch the film's blood
The lovers embrace, the death among the monkeys
Tonight's the night you meet, talk movies
All the way to her doorstep, then boom!
The big Hollywood kiss. More movies, more film
More cinema, more popcorn. You talk non-stop
Till dawn's early light. A slight disagreement over De Sica
I see, she says, You've the sensitivity of a pig. Slight
Has become big. You call. She's almost always out
When she's not, she's busy. You don't need *Western Union*
With Randolph Scott to get the message
Is life always a B movie with an unhappy ending?
You stagger like Brando in *On the Waterfront*
To the nearest theater. You fall into your seat
Muttering...is this the end of Rico?
Already you're feeling better
You're in the dark you love
The dark you've grown up in
The dark that lights your heart like home

## Talking Easy Thru My Hat

A-
Las, Mister
Giraffe
A Mo-
Digliani
Neck on s-
Tilts, in
Trudes thru
The window
Eats the flo-
Wers from my Ha
waiian shirt...
At that she almost laughed.
It'll be easy, I told myself,
Easy does it, just take it easy,
Speak easy, keep the pace easy,
Make the terms easy; it's an easy
Business to get into—being free
And easy; go easy into a kiss and
Then tell her how easy street feels
When the tin lizard, lounging on gr-
Een tires, licks the jam of traffic up
And over easy; keep the matter and the
Manner easy, for easy marks the man of
Easy living; yes, easy come and easy go
And may I say you are so easy on the eyes
And easy on the ego, you know, you make me
Wanna just take life easy in your easy chair...
Not there, she cried, You're too fat! Go sit on
Your hat...So I said, That's that and sat on my
Hat until it was flat...
Not much fun and easier said than done.

## The Promise

I'm not sad.
Don't believe my face.
...only waiting,
Asleep, you might say.
Don't worry.
I'll make my self
Up when I'm awake.
You'll see—
We'll have fun yet.

Ha, she said.

## Clear Light

Clear light
I promise to take care
To wake the sleeping petals round her eyes
And catch the smell of longing in her hair
Everywhere
Extraordinary air
Whirls from the music box of leaves
As thieves with magic steal
The fiery stars like kisses in the dark
To make a bracelet for her perfumed wrist
O sleight of hand
Unloose the lyrics of the heart
Match the trees...till wind-blown lady cries
The stars! The flowers! are singing in the fire

## Love's Thief

Night
Is a valentine
Of sky, wine-dark
Of moon sliced
Golden, a feast
And I
A thief in moonlight
Invited by the wind
Move beneath your window
Steal away
Among the trembling shadows
Of these branches, these leaves
And though I'm alone now
And have grown old
Mumbling in my beard
I still break for hearts
On this dark road
Still call out
In a clear voice
Your name...

## Moving Pictures

Walt and I started work today
Art curators, fancy titles for truck drivers
Moving pictures across this fat, flat land
Past repetition—the idols of electricity
And those secret gardens of cannabis
Known, only, so the story goes
To a thief who comes like a shadow
To reap in freedom what he sowed
Incarcerated, a guest of the state of Illinois
Hey, hey! The Caterpillar works
In a green field
Dip, says the sign
Stray Deer, another
The horses stand
Swish their tails
No
This first day
I'm not yet lonely
Without you

# O Listen to the Silence and the Words

O listen to the silence and the words
And the silence and the words and the silence
And the words and the silence...

All day held captive by the heat
Beaten, my mouth dry, and my tongue
Twisted into knots of nothingness
I need the stars, to sing
The gentle stars and night's erotic wind

Now jack-of-black-trades on top of the hill
Scooping up love in the pale moonlight
While a pure white cat on the lap of a saint
Curls the corners of my mind
Purring the burden of the dead

No need to ask
What drives me to dream
My eyes, my voice
Betray me...
Sex and death

0 listen to the silence and the words
And the silence and the words and the silence
And the words and the silence...and the words
And the silence...

## In My Cock and Bully Days

In my cock and bully days
On the beauty/beast express
When I'd run my reckless eye
And any old phrase would do
When thick as thumbs in the green
Thief wind, I made the round ground's
Spinning skin my house of joy
And the bouquets of poses
I would toss to the ladies
Were my flowers of black sunlight
Cracked through the rock

In the midnight of rivers
Where I washed out my virtue
Happy as a hobo
With his dreams in a bottle
No dog-haired saint in the fox-
Fire of God nor spellbound bee
In the dandelion's roar
Lived in the lovelight as I
And the heart, still shining, sings

## The Wait

Like a crack
In the sky
This tree
At the earth's edge
Fills my coffee cup
Coffee with whiskey
Half-gone now
Along with love
And the night
Razz rolls over, stretches
You talk in your sleep
My sad ear waits
For your waking
I scratch the dog
I keep the faith

## Hot Doggerel

Snoopy, Snoopy everywhere
This land's a doghouse of despair
How grand can Canyon feel
Using speech that's never real
Even Steven should retire
From Pentagonal quagmire
Wow, Love, now that we're hip
Can we do our comic strip?
O how soon will Sluggo be
Footloose and Nancy free?

## The Morning Dark

The morning dark
Is startled as some fly
That's round to buzz the door down
And wake us from our sawdust sleep
Succeeds or half-succeeds
So I assume since you're not moving
I'm the one who'll play the heartless part
The cruel hand of fate
There, I've caught the air and O!
That almost ghost reminds me
No more killing time and love
Today's the day I leave

## Sweethearts

Dead tread
Along the highway
Tires shredded like
Pieces of flesh, like
Sculptures of wild, dying birds
Of reptiles, stone-cold
Their now thin eyes hidden
In the hot sun
The risks are great
Bread, soap and O what flowers
On the seat beside me
Wildflowers
Picked for our bedroom
As I walked out the door
She called, I love you
I'll remember that, I mumbled
When I'm hit head on
It had happened once
A blur of blue...
I had given her a promise
When I slit my wrists
I won't do it in the apartment
Pretty melodramatic, huh?
Well, we're sweethearts
And I'm her best friend
For her
I'll keep my death
As bloodless as our love life

## Broadwater

In that broad womb of water where
What the croaking frog had spoken was no lie
*Daniel, you can't spend the rest of your life between my legs*
As often lacking grace I'd seek those remnants of forgiveness
And taste ashes on my sackcloth tongue
The sun shone on the breathing bed and wept
The telephone told a tale of woe
Ring, ring, ring, ring, ring, ring, ring...
Across the dark and bloody ground again

I pack my arguments and go

## Two Women

Love-soaked to the bone
Drowned in contention
Never together again
In the small of the dark
Violets keep
Tears run on time
Violets and tears together
Run
Soak and drown again

In the dark of the small
Bone of contention
Love never keeps

## The Freedom of Daughters

Can't you tell?
Transformed by your dwelling on it
I am the neglected daughter you were
Do you envy me my freedom
As I did yours and those girls' long ago—
Horses racing toward the hill, hoofbeats of joy
Out of the language of books children love
The woods turned golden and red, the breath
The beaded flesh, shining, startled into awe
By the grandeur in the sky
A flight of Canada Geese?
Once I heard them overhead
Stepped to the balcony
Above the stone where two hearts lie
And saw a third, my own
A broken image on a golden bough
Falling, still beating wildly
Then caged in hands
Yours, red with blood

## The Electric Poet

I entered her hidden apartment
As anxious as a cat smelling fish
Her white uniform with the gold buttons
Made me all the more militant
I marched past the dictionary
Humming a definition
A swingle is the swiple of a flail
Not even noticing the electric Royal Jetstar
With foot-long carriage and magic margins
I had given her to type my poetry
Because I never learned how
Was missing...
We began to live together again
Her lovely skin, the skin of my teeth
Hygienist by day, my typist by night
Yes, Jetstar was back; the keys were singing
The bell was ringing, but again it became
That same old story: get a job
Finally I packed up my poetry and
This time also my electric Royal
And left for Boston...very sad
But not really surprised
Everyone had told me
I wasn't her type...

## The Message

Brutal
She calls me
Remembers
Amid those cries
Of nightmare logic
All things broken
That had promised us
Felicity
Glass bones wood skin
Remembers
In case of emergency
Touch
Send the message
Past the madness
(O those terrible eyes!)
The hard transparency
Of the heart love breaks
Love enters

## Lucky in Cards

It's late; we're low on cigarettes
Finally the last card's played
Hurray for me
I can go to sleep a winner
I turn off the TV
Take the animals out back
Over the loose board's bang
Into what a magnificence
A night for believers in animism
Everything's so alive and the sky
A reddish blue. Why, are the stars
Wounded? Not even a flick of the head
In reply from the king of beasts next door
As silent as his relative, the Sphinx
He broods over the sleeping houses
While the other trees we walk to
Stand like his sentinels guarding the street
Along of course with the patrol car coming now
We don't see their faces; we retreat into
The backyard's geometry of sky and wire
Whose message comes through clear
Her promised call never came
O my little doggies
She done me wrong again
I go to bed a loser after all

## The Burnt Thumb

My woman
Whose name I can not divulge
For reasons of national security
Is lying in bed in the next room
Sleeping
I have just burnt my thumb
Lighting matches to see her lying
Naked in the dark
It is an image I can carry
With me forever
It is burnt on my mind
And my mind—for who can
Separate beauty from pain—
Is on my thumb
The same thumb I used to use
For hitchhiking
Now I hear the wild police sirens
I write, "Those goddam police sirens!"
Now I hear the faucet in the kitchen
Dripping
I write, "That goddam dripping faucet!"
Now I hear her turn in her sleep
And clear her throat
Now I write this down
"No freedom is as warm as your arms."
I decide to turn off the light
And return to bed
But first, I stare at my thumb
Now I take a poem
The first poem I ever typed
Crumple it up and throw it away
Here is the poem I crumpled up
And threw away
It is called, *"The Poem"*
  *The poem I wanted to write*
  *Or rather I the poem I wrote*
  *But didn't know I had written*
  *How like a little death*

*My leaving you*
I'm glad I crumpled it up
And threw it away
And burnt my thumb
The same thumb I used to use
For hitchhiking

## Asterisk

We spoke often
In the dark
Heart to broken heart
Turn after turn...
Once I gave you roses
To ease the pain
You bound my poems
You put a star on my name
Now my hand is silent
My tongue dumb
The world of work
The last rays of the sun...

Daniel

## Heart and Knife
*for Barbara*


To hell with the banks
And the damn bankers, the root
Of all evil:  the love of money
It's you, the banker's daughter
Who gets under my skin
Waiting for you
On my futon with Truffaut
With tuna and tofu
A monkey's tail of smoke
Curling round the lamp
Or in a car
High above the Cuyahoga
On one of those bridges
I'm thinking of jumping off
I begin to lose weight
The skin of the ghost
My fat chance
I wear thin
Down to the bone
Of our contention
Where true confessions
And the unsolved murders
Of schoolgirls live
How many stab wounds
Were found on Beverly Jarosz?
That's how many times
You've wounded my heart

On such sweet meat
My obsession feeds
Grows obese
O beast
Of unrequited
Love set loose
I want to make/unmake art
With heart and knife
Let go a barbaric yelp

Love betrayed
Your name is obscene
Who's listening?
Only the kitchen women
With their sharp knives
And grievances
Their ready eyes
Their hands
Red from sacrifice
All is loss now
All is grief
A shadow breathing dust
I pine away; a plain
Pine box, my own death
Floats to the stars
Even these words
Released like birds in the air
Hunger after silence...

## Sexist Love

She said to get
My shit & get out of
There, there, I said
Gimme time to get
My shit together
She said, Whether you get
Your shit together or not
Is not my problem
I need my freedom
Dumb me, I said
Shit & hit her & she hit me
And the shit hit the fan
Fanatic fantastic tock
Shit shock tit cock
O the hassle in the castle
Became razzle-dazzle
Just our foreplay
Wore us to a frazzle
And now, in this strangest of moments
As all the nights of mumbled love words
Become but dangerous flowers in a fist's boom-bah
Mocking turtledoves, knocked coup-coup de grace
Yes, suddenly, this free-ticket-to-Heaven tickle & shove
Makes death the next exit for reckless love...

## Too Old to Hope for Utopia

Too old to hope for Utopia
I carry forever the pain that is history
Forever to these rooms' strange accompaniment
Go naked words and the wordless wind
O listen, moon, soft as an eyewink
The tree of night trembling, leaf and star
You rap to my heart in original syntax
And pump to the brain in a new lovesong
Now blue sky pigeons' broken window
She calls to say her love is lukewarm
O where should I go? echoes the rainfall
What should I do? the storm thunders
I'll keep in the shadow of insect music
I'll go to the animal dark and hide
I'll follow the river back to the garden
And drown in the apples of eventide
And with me there'll always be a moonspun madness
And with me always...the lovemaking touch
I'll carry forever the pain that is history
And ever this stranger I must trust

## Sunshine

Sunshine and Happy Boy
Came into the office
Grabbed her, blindfolded her
Later they poured perfume on her
Later they stabbed her and she fainted
When I came back from Chicago
I gave her a broken guitar
Complications developed; she went into the hospital
I brought her champagne, marijuana, roses, chocolate
I told her I had a girlfriend; I told her
I still love you, and she cried
Now I call her my ex-ex-old lady
I'd call my girlfriend, but she's on vacation
Sunshine and Happy Boy are still at large
The broken guitar sits where I placed it
I'm alone now but enjoying myself
I've always wanted to write confessional poetry

## She

She sits
Reading catalogues
In the living room
Wishing she were rich
And could afford
The silver forgeries
Of the moon

She hardly
Touches me
Zero for spontaneity
She's bored
She won't believe
I've still some magic
Up my sleeve

Her mouth
Is moving now
I've heard
This all before
I know the words
By heart
In the heart's deep core
Home alone
With records on
She hums
Along
Is she wondering
What I'm doing
Where I've gone?

I'm dancing
On the ruins
Of the moon
A fool
With his shadow
To words
Without a tune

## In the Country of Blind Love

Straw on the grass
Dog on the straw
The stars are not gentle tonight
A full moon blooms without pity
All the wall falls
China and silence, broken
In this, the country of blind love
Am I the one-eyed, lonely King?
Once mirrored together, artiste and beggar
We sang to the ghosts of the ozone
Out hearts marooned on love's quixotic sand
The tale of the dog our cynosure
Now waves of darkness rain, the King is dead
The moon lies, a coin for the regal eye
Only words, quilled in the chill air
Strike and thrill. Arrows. Eros. Atage

## Famous in the Basement
*for Ginger*


Famous in the basement
My life in boxes
I lie listening to the stars
Those light years of silence
And from the white machinery
The rhythms of the sea
In this mildewed milieu
Love keeps a low profile
A sexual zero
On a futon dreamboat
Till heels overhead
The piano bares its teeth
And tout de suite
The avant-garde dog
Her soft underbelly
I try to rise, but
Gangplank panic
The heart keelhauled
The sundry arts jettisoned
I lose my toehold
On the cold linoleum
It's man overboard
Into doldrums of moonlight
As the dog makes her rounds
To lick my wounds

## That's It

1.
A place to brood
Is where I wish
To live
With the bare bones
Of the wind

2.
It's cool
In the forest
She said
In a dream
While I cried
My ordinary
Tears

3.
Here amid
The stones, the
Frogs, this night-
Mare freeze
I work my
Words from dark
To light, from
Dialogue to
Song...

## The Dream Thief

Who stole your dreams, what thief?
The street thief, the thief of late calls
The international thief of bail and hot sauce
The thief of hats, the thief of language and fish heads
The jaywalking thief, the thief of cigarettes and innocence
The mourning thief, grieving in rags and ashes
The thief of fire with socks that match, the clean thief
The thief of four dogs becoming five, the grand thief
With photographs and laughter, the thief of conscience
Blood on his hands, the film noir thief, the thief of rain
                                        and teeth
Didn't I, your thief of thieves, your dream thief
Those sleepless nights, mumble in the moonlight
Reach for the sky?

## Naked Women

More than the featherless bird
Beating the air with hammers
The naked woman with nothing up her sleeve
With no name nor any penny to that name
Wakes the white-robed morning
The winged heart of the bear falls victim
Out of the blue, without a prayer
To her sweet nothings and her brown hair
Dare he touch her beneath the chrysanthemums
Her elegant Arabian circling the foil?
No, no thieves in the night season
These zoo suitors at her feet. Look
The stars reside in their eyes
The armadillo, the buffalo, the camel
All praise the daily romance
The java hot on a low flame, the news
Of the world a blood-red, paper rose
For the other naked woman
Caught deep in the seaweed of dream
Her long-haired name spelled wrong
As often as Truffaut's, soft beside her
Our love beast. O I'd stay but must run
Just time for mere headlines and a kiss
When the Gypsy children want adventures
One sings, *Henry Hudson*
A song she knows by heart when dreaming
But forgets as the phone rings
There was a barn with rabbit hutches
A slide. If I'd slid down, she says
I knew I'd get my legs waxed
I laugh...I'm going to lunch with a Dr. Wax
What'll he say when I feed him the dream
I say, if her Polish legs were waxed
The hair would push outward as thick as wick
And Legs Klonowski, Madonna-faced in Paris
Would walk dreamlike through Notre Dame
Her liberated legs a myriad of shining candles
That barbarous act venerating our existential void

## Chocolate and Roses

We met and immediately
Wanted to be rich. That was a year ago
At last we've decided to pool our tears
Sell them to the International Salt Company
Become millionaires. What do we want
But a life of chocolate and roses
Steaks for Truffaut, our perfect dog
Trips abroad, candlelight suppers
New curtains for the bathroom
I'll feel so respectable, she says
Is that a bad feeling? I muse
I'd like a new image
Shave everyday, tie, stickpin
Shine on my shoes, spats, perhaps
Do you know how to jitterbug? she asks
Ah, what makes the heart leap
Its waters flow to a shining sea
We swim toward the bank and dally
Till the weather changes. Now
Out of hiding the fugitive sun
Announces the dream is over
We smile, stay broke
And settle into ecstasy

## A Love Note for Nancy

Dove of fire
With invisible child
Rising from the skull
Of a dog       biting on wood

Window-winged
Butterfly       light brown
Lighting on a knothole

Old man       crooked
But upright
Found long ago
Lying in grass
Gayblade smile

Two brick       rolling pin
Car spring poodle
Zigzag fireplug tree

Milton's toad
In the next room
Whispering to Eve
In a dream

Dark
Intransigent flower
Rusty swordfish
Dying of mercury
Brazed on a wave

Plus   of course
Muffles
And the rear bumper

Now let's see
You get all that
In my Duluth pack

## The Deadly Facts Of Love

The candle tells the keeper of the flame
Make light of darkness with a double dare
O what's the matter, gray, the skull is numb
Twice minus now your mother tongue and wit
You ran...stole the mourning from the dove
You made a refuge of the wailing wall
Now comfort thins and sorrow's under siege

It's true I brood wandering through these rooms
This is the perfect season for despair
Ancestral voices whirling in my ear
Yesterday's stark weather that went sour
Disharmony that split the lake and wood
And left me cursing, godless in the web
I grieve and know I cannot live on grief
I'd leave but O...where does a dead man go?

Go on mumbling, stumbling in the dark
A checkmate flowers in your buttonhole
Your ticking pocket, thief, she'll pick
She'll have you rubbing elbows with the crowd
Your shroud will be your working clothes and cap
By midnight you'll be fast asleep in bed
You'll learn the deadly facts of love outlast
The ghost in the mirror, the dream's bad blood

## Days without Dreams

Days without dreams
Night after night, the dark
No kisses, no hugs, no body
Next to body for 5, 6, 7 years
Who knows? Who can remember
How much time? The sentence goes on
This life without sex, nothing physical
Between us, everything material between us
Smoke and ivory, the gestures of sorrow
The narrow comfort of words, food, anger
I've blown up—a cartoon of flesh
At one with its own balloon thoughts
Moment by moment, born again
A wallflowering romantic, fallen in love
Howling like Humpty Dumpty
Bitter among the roses
When the moon is full
It all stopped years ago
Who knows now?
After the abortion
After the toxic shock
After my hands
Around her throat

## Two Loves

My all night heart
Stays open for another.
She calls to me in dream
Words from your sleep.
I answer, Yes, I know
You are the other;
The things you say
Are secrets I will keep
Until you two,
Becoming one, reveal
One is both the dream
Life and the real.

## For the Silence

Against the white wall
The arm fingertips to elbow
The hairs still wet from bathing
Slides easily the hand turning inward
Returns home touches down the coolness
On the white underside escaping
In the apartment in the bedroom
Of the woman with whom I've forgotten
How to be intimate there is a bicycle
Broken now lent to me in good faith
And working condition perhaps
It was the hard road I took
My weight that shaped
The pedals' demise twisted the handlebars
All my midnight errands gone awry
In her dream's deep
Does she bold as a mermaid
Swim toward the light
Of the cold unseen star
I wish upon
Sometimes
Words in a poem
Are only the preparation
For the silence

## Passion in the Red Room

The light in the red lamp
The full length mirror
Your reflection
The bed with the red bedspread
The blond easel, the unfinished painting
The smoke from your cigarette
My poem, the silence, the typewriter
The sound of your typing
Your blond hair, its red hue
Your arms, tanned, your vaccination mark
The red ash tray, the short red pants you're wearing
The red director's chair, its blond wood, your scar
And me in blue as usual
Fat...and soon to be abandoned

## A Bum Rap

So the talk's gettin' heavy
And I tell her, Listen, Nancy
I'm no good; I'm just a bum
I'm not even a good poet
You're not even a good bum, she says
Well, after that, I mean, after laughing
What's there to do but make love

## News from Home

The dogs have
Turned wild
Since you've gone
The moon blue
And my heart
In hell has fro-
Zen over.  It's
Heaven...
Your work is
Cut out for you
When you return...
All your calls
Have stopped
Save the mimes
And they're good
You can't hear
Them breathe
Otherwise every-
Thing's business
As usual
Only the blind
Want to read
Your poems
Only the deaf
Want to listen

## Distemper; or, Putting on the Dog

Like a dog with only
The moon for a bone
I've walked that yard
Of fallen acorns
Cocked a leg against oak
And angrily pissed away the time
Is that love? howls my dogged heart
Will jealousy hound me
Till I am mad in the manger?
Her bed's made and I'm not in it
To lie. O Love, bone dry now
Let me sleep

## Struck by Moonlight

Struck by moonlight
A rose up my sleeve
I am dying to abandon
These animal disguises
The wounded elk
The murderous ox
Nights move on the twitch
Of the pinball lizard
On the telephone madness
Of the uncoupled beast
Open the door
Ah, a frog fire of rubies
A Chinese, blue fish
Scaling the light
Deaf ears
Toward the muttering
Of the manic-depressive
Leap into sleep
In the electric cocoon
The bird harbored
In the nest of numbers
Chirps along
The fat caterpillar
Till out of the blue
French roast, croissants
Butter flies on toast
For you
My sweetheart of sheet music

## Look for the Lie
*for Nancy*


In the uncensored night
The froggy mind leaps
While the midfinger prints
A lovekiss
I loot the sky
Come away with the stars
And the moon
But of course
I always cocked about
Like I owned the night
And now
In the aftermath of love
(How many times did you come?)
You tell me more
Than I realized
And so often
That softens
The lie...

## The Devil's Mousetrap
*for NJB*


I just want the tactual facts
Deft fingers round the taddy prince of peace
The tickle of the hearth, its crackle
And the knack intact
To snap my devil in the mousetrap of her lap
As she goes down in fantasy with me
To sing of our enchantment by the sea
I started late and star-dark make my way
Am startled when the going goes for broke
Roughs up the heart and chases out the ghosts
These haunted feelings take time, touch and go
Milady kills or builds on what she knows
That fire works out the secrets in her soul
Now if I were by trade that journeyman
Who from a hat pulled tooth and nail, I'd soon
Abracadabra water into wine
And ride the devil's mousetrap to the moon

## Marijuana Moonlight

Ah, there we were
Feeling like movie stars
In Marijuana Moonlight
I told you I hadn't smoked in years
But the moon was right
And you laughed like you were my old lady
So I played you something old
To tell you I was ready
But you'd already played my oldness down
We're just winging it, you said
And led me through the moonlight
Across your waterbed

## O Miss Agony

*a Key West poem for NNR*


O Miss Agony
How thou had me barefoot
Running up thy tab, a madcap
Out of it & halfwit happy
At the slap of love
A sea street urchin, rapt in laughter
So hooked to the nook & granny of home
Turned seaman on the backrub bed watch
Facedown in houseboy black
O Miss Agony
Our Lady of the Bar Stools
How cool the Gethsemane rock
Which drew & jukebox quartered me
As my rough body that prodigal season
Tumbled hip & thigh in thy somersault sea
Then flash foreward: flesh
Flushed & coupled with the afterhours alcoholic dark
Was dumbfist struck, & blind alleycat eyes
Saw jailing tongue's wigwag
Had willy-nilly Delilah-cut
My wild & woolly bearded dove down
O Miss Agony
Quixotic change artist
Tilting at gin mills, promiscuity-bound
Who chases now with the goose on the loose
In the kidnapping wind, in the tattletale town?
For however that world without end amens
The agony is this: I miss the one friend
Whose fun with us thin-skinned, dues paying swingers
Fouled out flocking in the feathers together
O Miss Agony...

## Cheat Lake

Under the bridge where
You take me your cricket
Follows. The lake's on fire
With incredible roses. Plus
For me the sparkle, like letters
In old movie previews. My mind's
Empty of coming events, except
Footsteps: an invisible Astaire
Star-dances toward the shore

Did I cry out? There's no sound
But water. I move toward you
The light follows as if it were
My shadow. I reach you
Your head's in the clouds
You're barefooted. There are sharp rocks
Before us Love's grave lies, smoke & humor
We've enough rope, now, I joke, let's dance

## Freedom Rider Graffiti

Poem scraped with contraband
Fifty-cent piece on prison wall
In Parchman, Mississippi
Summer, 1961

Know now
No hero here
No how
If ever
Hung
On tree
The way
They done
JC
I'd be
Cross
I guess
Hell
Yes

## Street Poem
*for George & Jay*


In the wildwest night of the city
When the hot meet the cool
All she may ask is simply
Do you love or not?
Take your best shot
As for me, I've been re-created
Running the streets
I wear a gold tooth now
I go from bar to bar
I know the touch of the hustler
Beyond the touch
For she takes me under her wing
And we sail through the fog of money
We play the hearts of the city by ear
I like best the inviting variety of lights
Its promise of happenings always removes
The material weight of society from me
I move through beauty and through terror
Along the neon wall of night
A rag man coming home to light
Once I was singular in my disturbance
Now, good brothers, in my head are dreams
That cut like a knife. We need each other
Take care. It's in the air...

## Celebration

Out of the body politic dying
Nights without bread
Led to the carnival knowledge of color
At the nip and tuck of the budding revolt
In naked beard and scandalous sandals
I was overcome by the shallow, wee town
And contrary minds of the city sprawl
My mustardseed faith moved the mountain on me
And the flowers crushed on the sidewalks of time
Were my seedy bedpartners in crime
Rocks from the cradle and the billy club rub
Were wisdom cracking the star-spangled fang
After the dogbite the rabbis returned
With plastic priests and pastorized milk
So I wrapped God's news in an old fish story
...and man swung from ape's umbilical cord
Till guilt edged the serpent under the heel...
Bruised legacy and the bootstrap snapped
When all the innominate, hump-the-dump bones
Went grinding the stones and sticks to fire
While I Adamed an apple off the knowledge tree
And turning the other tongue in cheek
Slicked my good hair in her downhome desire
Then shifting to high gear in the wilderness streets
Where pot and panic handlers begged to differ
Of necessity tripping fantastic light
I turned on the system, the dark riders circling
Brother, can you spare a victim?
And moved on as thin as a praying mantis
...alive again: deadly as sin...
On the nit of my grit and the grin of my skin

## Repetition
*for Paula*


Every night from her tangled
Angle of love she would language me
Say something, she would turn and say
Say something
But I was the silence-is-golden one
Hiding my heart on the tip of my tongue
Seeking only to find in the act of love
A kind of animal dignity
If she comes, well, I thought
Leave well enough alone
No entanglements with words
No spoken promises to be broken or compromised
Alas, my animal kindness wasn't enough
She thought me heartless, returned home in tears
That was years ago. Now
As the night finds me alone
After another such hide-and-seek
My body remembers that golden love
Tears come, and on my silent lips
The words form at last...
Simple language, a simple act
And one I perform with dignity

## Of Loneliness and Kings

The King and I were born
In the same year
What you don't know is
Elvis died at birth
It was his twin that lived
And now this brother
The original Elvis impersonator
Has been sighted again
This time in Twinsburg
Among the twins
Looking more lonesome
Than Elvis ever did
Down at the end
Of Lonely Street
As lonesome as
Emily said Aretta was
Daniel, she's so lonely
She's glad when Jehovah Witnesses
Knock at the door
I was lonely, too
I knocked at the door
And shook my pelvis like Elvis
In the moonlight of her room
High on her erotic cloud
Above the crowded voices'
Illicit traffic in the street
Nocturnal walkers
Their black and sassy poverty
The bow-tie piety
Of *Muhammad Speaks*
And those layered nomads
With shaky carts
Pushing through the darkness
Their broken hearts
Yes, I was lonely, too
Born in the year of the King
And in the class of '52
Out of step at military school

Hoosier, Lutheran, ministerial to boot
I unresigned in the nick of time
Took back my first lieutenant bars
To go to the banquet
In blue suede shoes
Not to dance! To Lutherans
Normal dancing was a sin
And no one moved like Elvis then
Jesus was the King
I danced in my dreams
And wet the bed till sixteen
Quiet as a thief
My roommates asleep
I'd hang my sheets
Out the window to dry
After reveille
After the khaki rush
To line up, to salute
Not every eye would ride
The flag heavenward
Cadets at mess
(I was told later)
Full of toast and the Holy Ghost
Would pass along
The tongue-in-cheek news
Our dorm had surrendered
During the night
Yes, I was lonely, too
And like Elvis
Grew up in a land of Kings
The King of Jazz, the King of Swing
The King of Hollywood
*It Happened One Night*
In '34 with the King
Clark Gable and Claudette Colbert
And again that year
With Howard and Kathryn
Nine months later I saw the light
A light that filled
A thousand silver screens
And led me, grown-up

Deep into the dream
To the boyhood home
Of the Hollywood King
There I picked up a souvenir
A mere brick, then hocus-focus
Scissors, paper, stone
With a picture of Clark and Claudette
I threw that brick like a rose at art
A small icon to love on the run
Till the walls come tumbling down
And once, all at once
All the walls began to fall
Already a road scholar
Schooled in loneliness
I split with Angel for the coast
Ah, Angel
When asked whether he was white or black
Replied, Depends on who I'm with
And I took Whitman with us
Great-hatted, salt-bearded Walt
And read out loud *Leaves of Grass*
By sunlight in the open air
On the shoulder of the road
Where Angel, listening, winged it
And at night I read by streetlight
By moon and starlight, by passing-
Car light, by hand-cupped-round-the-flame
A flickering light, by construction-site light
That self-righting, potbelly torch
The road bomb, a sort of anarchist light
Whitman on fire fired us up
A true revolutionary poetlight
His army of words around us, his arm
He pointed the way, shouting
*Allons*! The road is before us
And calling us each, *Camerado*
And we knew this was the age of miracles
And he was our great Companion
Our King of the open road
And we would stick by each other
As long as we lived.

## Dear Enemy

Abandoned by women
Far from the heart under duress
In the deaf, deja vu moonlight
After the birth cries
The children spirited away
Into the thin air of strangers
Their painted blue skies, their caverns
Of luminous, handmade stars
I knew only to return to the road
To the theater of the world
To the movement to make heaven on earth
Naked, imprisoned as if in a mirror
Hungry, wanting to break through
The dream wounded
We bled into the headlines
And the evening news
Burning crossroads
Broken banjo in the dust
Where bodies sit, voices sing
We shall...We shall not...
Till redneck billy clubs swing
Flesh yields. Unloosed, blood flows
Head rocks and rolls. Stars appear
Stars and Bars, the long, wrong arm
Of the law, Jim Crow officer's awful
Caucasian rage, bird in a cage
Some of us wanted to know
if you were human
Well, hell, I'm thinking
It takes one to tell one
And Hell is everywhere
Up North the air fills, chills
With swastikas and flying bricks
Nightsticks, that dark forest
Moving like a river of pain
Like a trial of Job
Like a Biblical plague
Over the drumskin of the ghetto

Over the fires on the plain
Now keep a sick, white crowd at bay
Don't ask who they are
Wearing these savage masks
Just average is savage
Beaten back, driven
From the edge of the crowd
They come back, again vulgar
Loud, resilient as rope
Full of hope as a lynch mob
And still the nightsticks do their job
Keep us marchers on the move
Through the hostile neighborhood
Till out of frustration
And, I imagine, to their sorrow
Those desperately against us
Realize they must borrow
A page from our demonstrations
Cool their rage, move ahead together
And sit peacefully in the street
O sweet Jesus! What a red-letter moment
Of history, a moral victory, an epiphany
In a crisis our enemies act just like us
Using our own non-violent tactic
To stop us in our tracks
And how do we respond
To this rendezvous with irony
To this gift of non-violence
From those who hate us?
We wait in silence
As if struck dumb
Even our Preacher, bruised
Whose words rang out
Against the first stone cast
Now holds his tongue
No talk of dialogue nor reconciliation
No mention of redemption of the nation
The only sound—
Nightsticks on flesh and bone
Them stumbling, shouts, crying out
Trying to run in panic, in pain

Dear Enemy, dark with blood, your face
Is our unbroken mirror. The way is clear
The dogs bark and the Movement moves on...

## Black Is the Color of Anarchy

Am I that bum
Who thumbs from Cleveburg to Chi Town
Comes in a rush of fools to Rush Street
Reads poetry at an eatery with Joffre?
Hallelujah, good friend Joffre
His sword beaten into a plowshare pen
Tilts in the Windy City
At the dark conspiracies of the age
Balances his rage with his matchless laugh
His rude pockets burst with info
But hold no folding legal tender
He trashes cash in the same flames
With the red, white, and blue
Or any flag of state
For flags mean business
And business means war
And war means the poor
Go from rags to ditches
And in the last ditch
You sing or die
So on a nightstick night
Under the wild onion moon
He sings out poems of Anarchy
While at his feet
Like hounds round a fire
His bags are as comfortable as you
Who may desire to weigh this knowledge
Joffre, sedentary among his friends
Or hoofing it down these streets
Alone, carrying his own black silence
Is his own black poem

## In County Jail
*for a Walter Shields painting*

When justice
Is a railroad
Is the freedom train
Mere dream
This tear here
The ticket
The destination
Pain?
What travail to travel
Trials that never end
Freedom's
The air I want
To breathe again
Cold bars! These tracks
My time's runnin' on
Cold as the cash
I lack, cold as
The stars I wish upon
Each day to stay human
To hold on, to let go
I fly home
To your arms'
Sweet freedom
I touch your face
I wake...

## The Naked Truth
*for Emily Campbell*


The Emperor has no clothes
And being so exposed
He seems to lose his dignity
O alas, alack!
Too bad he's not
Black and beautiful
Like our Emily
When she disrobes
And holds a pose
It seems to enhance
Her dignity
Nothing's left to chance
The artist can glance
And paint his own fancy Emily
But O, the soup is hot!
Mrs. Campbell's not
Getting equal pay and so
She must do her thing
And like Dr. King
Walk 'round these walls
Of Jericho

## Would You Write a Poem about Me?
*for Marlene*


Would you write a poem about me?
I like music, death, numbers & jewelry
I'm gonna write books, the first one about love
The second about my life 'cause it's very interesting
One night I composed a 2,000,000-word Declaration
Of Negro Rights but I couldn't write it down 'cause
I didn't have a light bulb; sure wish I had a light bulb
That night...you'd have really liked it
I can write good love letters; they might be mushy
But they mean a whole lot...I do things the way I feel
You know, they wanted to give me $500 just to dance nude
Sshhh, I bought 4 copies of that record & I don't have one
                                        for myself
You know, they tried to kill me. You wanna marry me?
I mean, you wanna be my boyfriend, yes or no?
I like Eye-talian men mostly. Don't put all that in there
It's personal, well, give me a light. What sign do you think
I was born under? What are you, Aquarius? Aries?
I'm Libra, the scales balanced. Anyway I'm leaving tomorrow
I'm supposed to have got my senses back. It took fourteen men
To lock me up last time; they said I bit the supervisor's nose off
They'll tell lies on you. Sometimes I buy music just for the words
Do you know any languages? How do you say *I love you* in
                                        English?
Will you live with me? We'll have everything; I'm on Welfare
Do you write in shorthand? I can't read it. I'll have to give you
Lessons on how to write. Come here for a second...X...
Good night. Call me tomorrow. I'll be free as a bird

## Beyond the Dream

Astonished by trees
The bird woman stands
Drinking rain
Passages from the King James
Whirl through her head
All her worldly goods
In shopping bags
Her dream book, her day-old bread
Sway as she goes on her crooked foot
To the door of a newfound friend
On whose couch she unbends
Into a watery sleep
When she dreams, she flies above
What matters on the street
The honking cars, the hookers
To the treetops and speaks to the birds
Who take her breadcrumb words
Beyond the dream to Jesus

## Am I Blue?

Am I blue
As blue as
The sky that falls
Once in a blue moon
Leaving traces
On these trees
These blue woods
Where the man
With the blue guitar
Losing his way
Points the guitar
At the far North Star
And plays the blues
Till he's free?
Am I blue
As blue as
That blue streak
Of anger
Freedom's great
Wave to save
Each endangered tree
Between the devil
And the deep blue sea?
Am I that true blue
That free?
Once
When Liberty Boulevard became
Martin Luther King Drive
A troubled woman of color
Beautiful, alive, naked
Save for a patch of blue
Over her pubic hair
Stirred the air
Running without a word
Down the double yellow lines
A magnificent act
That seemed to say
At the same time

Free, free at last
Thanks God almighty
I'm free at last
And
Am I blue?

## Red Sky

Sleeps not
Like a rock
On St. Peter's
Sidewalk, Robert
Stinks to high heaven
Fully clothed, clutching
His crutch under a blanket
Or two, wet from his bodily
And the weather's fluids
Does he dream he's running
Naked in Africa's sunlight?
Awakened, puts two fingers
To his lips, the international
Sign of nicotine need
This morning, though, I've
Nothing save pastries and water
Quit smoking, I joke
That's why one leg's
Shorter than the other
Near him in a crouch
A street warrior brother
Wearing a thin blanket
As if it were a cape
Is shivering, nods no
To my offering of day-old
In the jungle of the city
Shakes no spear, moves
In no sphere of influence
Speaks only truth
It's too cold to eat...
His words lend ballast to silence

The sky is red with warning

## Fruit of the Loon Trilogy:
## Apple, Orange, Banana


You've
A lovely
Voice
Madam
The kind
Of voice
One might
Have heard
In the garden
Before the Fall
A voice calling
Come, Adam
Eat

Warren G
Harding's
Orange e-
Asy chair
Smile disappeared
In the snow
Like Napoleon's
Russian dream

Under her dress
Mrs. Freud
Wore a banana

# Rats

Black Checker Cab midnight
Memorial Day Eve downtown
Deborah Campbell feeds the poor
Veterans of the street and the latest trickle
Down and outers of our one nation indivisible
Watch out! There's more humankindness on the move
Deb goes for blankets, tells me the rats of Public Square
Are biting the hungry who are homeless there
Rats! I say to myself, Rats! Give 'em cheese
Federal cheese. Why should they risk
Getting a disease from biting the poor?
Sure, get them little darlin's
Out of their ratholes rat-a-tat-tat
Clean 'em up, mainstream 'em, get 'em jobs
In laboratories testing products, smoking
Let 'em be all they can be in the Army. Boom!
Send 'em into space ... to the moon with Alice
For God, green cheese and country. Give 'em the vote
Every vote counts and like everyone else who votes
Count on them to keep the fat cats in power
Hallelujah, let them be free, let them eat brie
And pay through the nose to get those hot tickets
For the Pied Piper of Hamelin's American tour
Forget the poor. They don't give a rat's ass for America
Or anything. Yes, it's time to get the rats into the rat
race

# Daniel

This star I caught
Years ago, this
Falling star that
Fell like a tear
But became like
A steady flame
Above the i
In my name
Take it for the
Sky of your i
Make it your own
It may be the thing
That brings a smile
To someone you love
Miles from now
When you're a
Far cry from home

**Daniel**

## A Morning Reflection

Witness the whiteness of daylight
Through the Venetian blind
Reflecting in the room on the glass
Of the Matisse nude. It exactly
Covers her below the navel with a light
Touch of modesty as if the artist himself
Had returned during the night
To lay a bed sheet there. Her breasts
Are a fraction above the direct gaze
Of my now awakened eyes as she lies
Inviting me, as it were, inside the frame
Left leaning, perhaps by chance, against
The wall. O just call me a low character
On a futon—someone who contemplates
Artfully rising to step naked again
Into another shining, half-Puritanical day

## In the Silence

Trees gnarled
Against the night sky
Truffaut
Sits on the snow
A statue looking up
At what so intensely
So doggedly
An elusiveness
The ubiquity of the oneness of things
The question mark is lost
Light as a white feather
In the silence
In the fallen snow

## Rude Early Morning

Rude early morning, leapfrog wind
Fly the mind to the leafless tree
Threadbare hands pick the pockets for heat
While the nose follows the hard smell of snow
And the sky is blue and white and gray

Rude early morning, churchbell wind
Are friends still dressed in Sunday sleep?
Look in the windows, rap on the door
Who's there? It's me. Well...please go away
And the sky is crooked and black as sin

Rude early morning, bone-cold wind
Rush the heart down streets where I grieved
There a lone sparrow in the truth of snow
Says, Hello? and I say, Good day
Good day to all lovers still hot on the trail

And the sky is new...bright and gay

## That We are One

That we are one with the dumb
And stumble with the halt
And blindly tap messages in the infinite dark
Of little faith or too much, that soon
The fly-by-night caught in the sweep of the broom
Turns up a thorn in our flesh and blood streets
And follows us home to our room

That we are run by the gun
And commanded to halt
Or blindly track savages in the animal dark
Of little love or too much, that soon
The dove that plucked the green leaf from the ruins
Returns from the fire black as the raven
And grieves as we weave our own doom

These truths, hard as nails
Are hammered in hands
That bleed in jails across the land

## Waiting for the Judge

After the interviews
We wait for the judge to arrive
The defendants in their cells and I
Wandering outside the station
My eyes on the ground
A rubber band
Fallen into the shape of a heart
And my shoes
I was alright when I left home
But now I'm wearing one brown
One tan
Luckily in my car
I find a pair
Black
In good condition
Though green with mold
These
Like the ones I have on
Belonged to my father
I wipe off the mold
With an old newspaper
Change and wait
At the heart of justice
Is a waiting
Which fathers injustice
Turns hearts into mold
And hope as black
As these heirlooms on my feet
Or a judge's robe

## In the Shape of a Gun

I've had two readings
Cancelled by the Workhouse
The officials
At the House of Correction
Are always correct
I *was* going to read
My escapist poetry
Maybe that poem
In the shape of a gun
O Apollinaire
With a little polish
Would work as well
As Dillinger's bar of soap
Or did the hand
That held the pistol
As a lover holds a flower
Whittle it out of wood
And iron will?
Or as some scribes
Allege, John
Justice had been
Served...a bribe
No look-alike
But the real thing
Took you
To the road
And home

**Soup Poem d'Jour**
*for John Cook*


Me so angry
Me so hungry
Miso lentil
Ahhh
Me so gentle



**Culture**


After
*The Dying Swan*
In 1911
Pavlova's dogs
Were tired

## We are All Gunmen

Cross at the light
And step over the dead
We are all gunmen
After the trial
The judge said, Daniel
You can say anything
You want to in America
But you've got to pay for it
We are all gunmen
I heard it at the C-Saw
The time the Angels trashed my reading
After the poets'll come the niggers
We are all gunmen
How many killers are out tonight?
How many good Germans
Are threatening your life?
We are all gunmen
We are all gunmen
Let's put the L back in FLAG
Chirps our sweet songbird
Turned dark bird prey
But pray tell, Anita Bryant
What do you need?
You're it in the game of nuclear tag
Hey, hey, Enola Gay
How many nukes in the old bomb bay today?
I mean, how many dickheads with warheads?
How many pricks?
We are all gunmen
We are all gunmen
We're big brains. We're scientists
We got the grants to prove it
Star Wars. Shee-it
Let's knock those monkeys' brains out
The planet of the apes can go to hell
We need better helmets for the NFL
The whole country can go on the dole
We're gonna meet Russia in the Super Bowl

We are all gunmen
We are all gunmen
No less than Thomas Jefferson said
We are all gunmen

Cross at the light
And step over the dead
We are all gunmen

## Red Cleveland

The color red along the highway
The steadiness of taillights, the passion
Of advertisers, red's ubiquity in signs
Tooth and nail, the bloody tracks of predators
Buildings ablaze, we are dazzled by this red-letter night
Is that a neon rose tattooing the brick?
Red flags of warning, red ball express
Incendiary cargo, the fugitive arsonist
His patriotic gas, the money in his pocket
Bursts into flame, the red ghost ranges
Over the lost wilderness, traffic stops in the name
Of lovely red...Chase Brass and Copper...Zagar
But O my favorite, this yellow darkening into red
Delicious sun the peach I eat

## Wild Onions

In those inevitable nights
When the sounder of swine
Playing to the hilt
Spills the milkwhite pearls
Into global living rooms
When in the ear of our Lord
The Word is found
Beating like a drum
Truth crushed to the ground
Will you stand out
In that reign of terror
Sabres rattling tooth and nail
And join the daisy chain to jail?
Now all who know the maiden rage
Smell hard the flowers' blood
Who scan the age can diagram
The sentences of the judge
Or turning inward still may reach
Through zigzag arguments' dark
The wild romantic heart

# The 23ʳᵈ Skiddoo

The Warlord's the shepherd I shall not want.
2 He maketh me to lie; for more West land
he bleedeth me; besides the till, what matters?
3 He boreth my soul; he feedeth me the jazz,
our might is righteous, for his games' sake.
4 Yea, yea, yea, though I walk through the valley
of the Jolly Green Giant, I will fear
know evil: for thy CIA is with me:
thy rod and thy staff they pacify me.
5 Thou preparest a statement for the press
on the presence of mine enemies: the
Vietnamese in Vietnam, the Che's
Lounging below the border, the Raps in
the traps, the Hippies on trips, the sheepskin
Doves, and that other Yellow Peril: thou
appointest a HHHead with oil on thy
tongue: thy cupidity runneth over.
6 Shirley Temple and Hershey shall swallow
me and all the lives of my day: then who will
dwell in the House and Senate of LBJ forever?

## Coventry

Fast-as-molasses Seymour
Works at County Welfare
Lives alone, in his rooms
Books, a tape recorder
Temporarily out of order
While around the corner
Are the wife & daughter
In their genteel squalor
Living better thru electricity
Color TV, a new dryer
Watch the trash get higher
Watch the dust gather round the broom
Beard, ash & glasses Seymour
Play that damn piano
Then eat your supper with a spoon
After soup & crackers
Like a couple of characters
We'll go out & act
As crazy as a loon
We are going gambling
Drinking & exploring
Going to the C-Saw
Irv's, the Saloon
Fast-as-molasses
Beard, ash & glasses
We are going to Coventry
To howl at the moon

## The Night Season

A change of weather
Again the winds of war
Bring in the night season
As in childhood when I looked
Into the glass heart of grief
The blue stars daily turning gold
I wondered whether
And with what grace
I might grow old
Now I only know
Some are wise by dreamlight
Each newborn day a wish come true
And you
Coming from the dark
Standing by the window
In your room
Are part
Of a string of hearts
Wishing a shower
Of shooting stars
Would bloom
Like thousands
Of flowers
For peace...

## If Light were Music

If light were music
The night earth spinning
Toward its golden star
And in that turning
The echo of the moon
On the water reveals
The killer in the mirror
A shadow breathing hard
Whose dark weight
Pitches on the shore
Whose heart of glass reads
In case of emergency...break
If light were language
Spoken only in tongues
By hearts on fire
The wordless eye would sing
Its blind desire; forgiveness
Would flow like blood
If light were sound
Natural to the ground of all beings
Would each creature cross the field
To comfort each in the deep dreaming?

## In Love's New Light

When the good weather comes
And the freeze round the rude red ball
Natures into green and all our dreams
Bear witness to our laying our burdens down
I wake my love and, naked, snake
Freckle to mole to tit and hiss: This is, this is
This is it
When Revolution comes
And marks on workers' backs
Rise up and crack the whip into
A school for social change
So all our marks are lovers' marks
Then nothing Love may say to do is foolish
Or is strange
When Death comes
Sleepy-eyed and sheepish round our door
His wolf fangs caught and muzzled
In his mumbling beard
Then call the beggar in, treat him as a friend
For all our scapes in Love's new light
Are graced with charm again

## How Poets Live

Now to discard the skin of darkness
Of the cellar where I dwell on ambiguity
Up the stairs I rise to wake the moon
Out of its cold beauty sleep, the ghost snow
On the lawn inviting me to live the life
Of children in the light, in the garden
Like desert nomads, the white garments falling
Through the branches of the tree into a state of grace
No sacrifice of an Isaac nor a ram caught in a thicket
Integrates our hearts. Only this, to awake to dream
Can take us beyond our nostalgia for the new
And teach our children how poets live
Mouth to hand, hand to mouth, silent as light

# Three

## "The Ancient Longing to Belong"

## Old Willie Belle Pruitt

When Willie Belle Pruitt met me, she said
You've got the picture of Jesus in your face
But Jesus! The pictures I had in my head
The hoses...the dogs...moments of fire and grace
What happened once in Bethlehem
Happened again in Birmingham
The innocent children dead
Now sometimes a name hurts worse than a stone
Sometimes a bone breaks like a stick
Sometimes what happens happens alone
Suddenly life is cut to the quick
O Willie Belle Pruitt, who buries your dead?
Eyes untutored, hands unschooled
Sleeping on the floor of your sister's shack
You rise from the shadows, pass the lilies of the field
In the black night of sorrow, a sparrow on the wing
To go to mass meetings, to march in the streets, to sing...
They beat you. I cry out. I bleed
For I am bound to you
Just like a tree
That's standing by the water
We shall not be moved
Your pain
Is my name, too

## A Valentine for Mother's Day

Lazy to ladies and their nightmare ways
I pitched fullbelly on the rosy spit
Raised Cain's mark with my scapegoat smell
And plunged pellmell in the white whale's pit
On her wrists she had written her hardluck piece
Our game name is Alice with a dull breadknife
And again as I entered her no exit life
She said, Here's the beast with the bad, black breath
And gave up money as the tongue petered out
Across the wires her catcalls crawled
Between the cockcrows when the pratfall came
No one and everyone was there to blame
For waxwings stumped on the hairs of the sun
And Christ's double cross on the scarecrow's pole

**K**

This is the country of those gone mad
The crickets building time bombs in the grass
To tick away eternity; and see the black cat scat
From crucifixion on the cross-eyed path
Else, cradled like a manchild in the moon
Mice in the feet and cheesecake on a spoon
I cannot sleep: blind with a love of night I keep
One eye open for the thief who caught the falling star
Locked her ashes in a jar, and now is calling me...
While in my lazy ear I hear world news from the rocking chair
That old redhead with a blue tattoo and a dim-eyed dog
                                          named Sam
Yes, now's the time to act; so listen, here's the plan
We'll have no pity; we'll spend the night out
In the electric city and Death will lead the band

## His Second Coming

I used to borrow sorrow from the world
Read history and become inflamed
Now I lay my longings on the grass
And chant to ants some trouble of my own
There's a monkey upstairs underneath a lamp
He sits all day and stares at a skull
Above a woman staggering in her sleep
Our eighty-one year old Grandma at Death's door

The days of grace are running out of breath
I go to town and walk along the shore
I see the ships and fishermen who sit
And stare all day at water, sky and rock
I think of women, soft, who offered love
The wood I knock on quickly turns to stone
No sandals on the waves, I must get home
His second coming's tattooed on the wind

## The Universe is Coupled to the Core

The universe is coupled to the core
The match that broke the serpent's back
And lit the flaming sword is my torch, too
The Word that in the womb gave form to ooze
That set the syllables ticking in the skull
Says language and the blood are one and all
The letters of our sex explode the brain
And sharpen into fate our acts of love

Dead faces in the hands still rule the day
They measure out the traffic to the grave
The mirror cracks and slivers in the soul
To every morrow of our crooked age
Ah, Woman in the crossfire of your room
Entertaining King James on your bed
His verses leap and catch you by the heart
You cry out...and the world gives you a stone

Now no strategic air the bones may breathe
Down long green walking streets of time
Can shake the dog-eared silence into song
Or take the salt of sorrow from the wound

## My Alma Mater

May fourth, four more dead, another march
Coffins by candlelight; the slaughtered innocents
To be buried in effigy; Jesus-faced carpenters
Doubling as pallbearers: arts & crafts in the vanguard
Of the Revolution—in a homemade coffin, a homemade
                                                victim
Old clothes stuffed with rags, a shiny plastic American flag
Our scars & stripes forever, the death mask
Faces—familiar—flicker by; stars scatter & hide
A few flowers around our make-believe corpse
Make me think again: the final death of flower power
Talking over the open graves: what can be said
That hasn't been said, that hasn't already been said
My Lai, Cambodia, Black Panthers
And now, hard to believe, my alma mater, Kent State
O America, cold machine in high fever
Why must you devour the young?
In the early morning tenderness
The tears for our dead mingle with the dew
The victory bell rests in silence
That ringing in the ears?
Merely the echo of gunfire

## All Night

All night the streets are mine
Bits and pieces of shattered light
And far off against the caverned sky
Stalagmites of the burning city
But I am one to wander close to home
Find a path that twists between the trees
To a silver dollar and near the bank
Catch the stream in its flux and ease
Did I say dollar?
More often it's simply change
Any way I get my money's worth
Motherless now
I feel I need
A deep connection with the earth
With all the night forces that call and beckon
In this dark kingdom of lovers and thieves
Sanctuary for a man of words
O look
This pocket where I hid my heart's been picked

## Orville

A travellin' day in Illinois
The pigs root in the sunshine
Walter says
I'd never raise anything
I knew was gonna be killed
Walter, my brother-in-law
Had a brother named Orville
They were raised on Chicago's Southside
Where Orville died in captivity
In the custody of the Police
Charged with reckless and drunken driving
The question was raised at the inquest
Was it murder?
No, Pig-lovers, Justice prevailed
Just as you might expect
They ruled: sooey-sooey-suicide
He hanged himself in his cell
Just another Black drop
In the Whitewash of America

A travellin' day in Illinois
Highways 80, 34; the wind blows
The pigs root in the sunshine...

## My Old Man

To die in San Diego
In The Veterans' Hospital
Amid the tubes & masks
The people were nice, the doctors young
This is the life, he said
I'm so shrunk up
I can't find my peter
To die in San Diego
At the end of the rainbow
The Airstream sits
In the trailer court
Waiting to be sold
To another American dreamer
To die in San Diego
With a voice like Brando's
In *The Godfather*
With a picture
Of a nude woman, my dead mother
Stuck away in his important papers
With *Good News for Modern Man*
On the hospital night stand
To die in San Diego
California
My old man
Worked all his life
In those dark, Satanic mills

& I loved the smell of his grit

## The Anatomy of Love

When Love comes out the window
The Law goes in the door
They want to know what was that sound
Love, he says she said
All the way down
He lies, Sadd says, I fear foul play
Love's love was a rope of sand
And that was the wrong way, Corrigan replies
To let the lovelight in her eyes
We charge Love with a felony
I disagree, John T, says Love's attorney
Love's love was grand; it just got out of hand
Why, Dave was Adam, Virginia Eve
Their only sin, originality: she dangled
Like forbidden fruit three stories high
And then she fell...and then she died
For what shall Love be tried?
O I supposed if I'd been Love
I'd have kept that window closed. Who knows?
When Love goes out the window
The Law comes in the door
They know it when they hear that sound
Love, he cries she cried
All the way down

## Aunt Martha

Flying to Washington, D.C.
To Aunt Martha's funeral
Looking out the window
Down at the world
I don't care whether I live or die
Says the man who quit smoking
You out there
I don't care whether I live with you again
Says the man who eats licorice
Someone will take care of my dogs
Someone else will get the poor out of jail
Says the man who drinks coffee after coffee
Black as the day's humor
I, too, will be free
Says the man who chews bubble gum
Aunt Martha
Says nothing

## Death and Dogshit

I thought I had arrived
A tab at a bar, a friend's place
Where we so-called Street Poets
Could read as often as we wanted
My friend was blown away
Again the Street won
Since then I think I've been
Drinking more and my life
When I care to look at it
Seems as senseless as his dying
And what do you see
On the horizon, Mr. Thompson?
Death and dogshit
And where is it you're going
Mr. Thompson? Out, into the night
In fact, with three wanton women
Married mothers: Frye boots and
Marijuana, apple pie and orgasm
And what is it you want, Mr. Thompson?
Me and my three very literary ladies?
A last call
One more round
Safe passage through Hades

## The Shadow Knows
*for Walter*


It was simply a case
Of post nose-job depression
Also the moles had been removed
From his backyard where he went out
That afternoon and dribbled himself to death
With a visiting basketball. Because he was a suicide
The Catholic Church refused to bury him
That didn't bother him
Since he was dead and had been raised Pentecostal
And his wife Lutheran
Fortunately he died with an erection
His wife had a special casket made
For an open-fly ceremony
She wanted everybody to say good-bye to the prick

## Razz's Poem

Your death
Smashes our clock
The cold nose of morning
And the evening walk
Praise waters
That flow
Through our eyes
Through the park
Praise fires
That glow
In the heart
Of the dark
Praise winds
That blow
Our ashes
Our love
To the earth underfoot
To the skies above
O gutter moon chrome blood
Animal grief I
Must woo
The broken voice
Hanging on the wire

# The Birdman of the Workhouse

For weeks we watched the eggs
Four speckled eggs, a nest in the grass
Beyond the diamond. Alone or with a friend
Almost daily by the ember light of evening
Especially on the weekend when we'd walk more
We'd check on the eggs
Some of us, confused, maybe just fooled by nature
Couldn't remember exactly where they were
Anthony, an old alkie with whom I played rummy
Confessed to me he never could find them
I took him near the fence and showed him the high grass
You can always tell, I told him, I cut around the nest
Once I'd come up on the mother sitting there
When I got close with the mower, her tail feathers rose like a
                                                              cat's fur
I thought of the eggs as special. I cautioned the other cutters
Inmates were already calling me The Birdman, because of
                                                              the breadbox
For the birds I'd set on the dining-room table
After each meal I'd scatter the scraps in the yard
Sometimes an anonymous bird-lover would beat me to the
                                                              bread
Friday the eggs were gone Saturday I had to cut in the yard
                                                              again
Stanko's cousin came running over to warn me
The eggs are gone. I told him
They've hatched, he said, we've seen them
So you gotta watch out for the nest
Wow, that's great. But there's no nest, I assured him
Sunday morning Al, a good talker, and I were walking
Al spotted them first. Two dead baby birds
Flattened—as if run over by something
I got a paper cup, scooped them up
And put them in a big hole near the fence
The same hole one of the joggers had stepped in
It took time to sink in. I didn't want to face it
Just like Vietnam, I thought

## The Last Tattoo

Sweet Ravenna
Evening jail talk
Playing spades talk
Hey, man, how come
You got a tattoo
On your back?
You can't see it

My woman likes it

I know a dude with a frog
On the end of his dick
He whips it out
Every time he sees ya
He did five years in Mansfield
I'm gonna get me one
Right in the crack of my ass
Just four letters
K-I-S-S

Tony Walsh
An old friend from Kent State
Now one of the Coalition lawyers
Told me in the courtroom
Before we were sentenced
Daniel...get up there and say
Up the ass of the ruling class
Nooo, I said, my proctologist told me
To quit giving assholes a bad name...
K-I-S-S, Judge, here's the last tattoo
The dead are my defense. Their silence

## The Heart's Cargo

Awake at last past Liberty's
Long snake of warning
Winged apocalypse
Gull scatter and wind
Our sulking wounds traffic
Toward the downtown spread
Sky rocks the eye
Does each white horse cry
Help me, I'm dying?
Light and lungs shake loose
Vessels, feather and scale
Pitch to the elements
What crane can wrestle
With the heart's cargo?
Above the black-wreathed stadium
A cloud of sorrow, the Indians' sign
No home runs cheer Chief Wahoo
Only memory's running home grief
The face cracked open on the bridge
The tears flowing over the Cuyahoga
Come home, Daniel, your mother's dead
I fell in with the dreaming crowd
We worked the games a winning season
A hot dog lady, an orangeade kid
With no place like first place
No place like home
Still our harbor for dark desire
Now its victims wait
For my shoulder against the stone
Up the hill, trudge
To the halls of justice
In the distance gulls circle
Like buzzards over death

## William Hart

Don't look for Peaches
In the inner reaches of the city
Sitting pretty or shaking his hips
The way he once did on the strip
He's gone for good
Only his shadow dances
Where the street poor
Take their chances
Amid the breadcrumbs and the blood
That day the pigeons lost Hart
Their friend, and cried
The Monarch butterfly
I'd found on the sidewalk died
And I wondered whether
Their souls winged heavenward together

## Naked Hearts

When my mother
Sunbathed on the roof
Planes would sometimes
Buzz the house

On an afternoon
At home after her operation
She was proud
Vacuuming the rug
Naked
Of her lone breast
And her scar

Out of her mind
In a time of violence
(O forgive me, Mother
My brutality)
She ran from the trailer
Out of the camp
Without a stitch on
In time
To wrestle home
The angel of death

A tree
Or a whole forest
May have fallen
The night no human woke
To hear her dying breath
After that
My life in pain—
Wounded, aggrieved
Dejavued by love again
A breakup
Leading to a breakdown
To my endless
Manic panic pacing

In the empty apartment
Suddenly
I found my mother
In the dark
Cave of sorrow
And spoke to her
Naked heart
To naked heart

## Mourning Oatmeal

Dream basement dark
No rat scurry just
Earth rasp and shudder jinx
Birds unload morning
Behind garbage ruderal
Pickup machine beast rhythms
Natural as gearbox light
Lo, air clock workers
Up
Dog absence profound
Want dream back
Want howl turn
Spiderweb liquidity steps
Surprise
No cheeky tongue shines
No internal eyewinks balance
Only déjà voodoo

## Frieda Gold

A cacophony of experts
Speculate on television
What life will be like
In the nineties
Why don't they ask me?
Says Frieda with a sly smile
I'm already there...
You clean
You cook
You prepare
Seder for Pesach
For sons
Four questions
Forever
The bread of affliction
Broth, bitter herbs, an egg
The open door...
Why is this night different
From all other nights?
No Elijah nor Messiah
To drink the wine
Death comes instead
Everywhere forests are dying
There's a tear in the sky
Oil on the waters
A letter written with love
Unsent
Canceled by the morning call
In a drawer slightly ajar
Coupons no one will redeem
What can be said
In the darkness save
Sorrow. Sorrow. Sorrow. Sorrow
Sarah, Rebecca, Rachel, Leah
The circle widens to let in Frieda
Again as sons
The brothers have gathered

And the earth
Is shoveled in anger
Herb, Sid, Eugene, Bob
Brothers in affliction
What alchemy
Has turned the moon
Golden? It beckons
Offering
The solace of light
The way home...

## May 4

Though I come with passion to Kent
I cleave to Cleveland, oil and steel
The ghosts of John D. Rockefeller
And Margaret Bourke-White
Our river in the Flats, the Cuyahoga
A river remembering its fire, still running
Crooked as a politician past the foundry
Where the honorable statue of James A. Rhodes
Complete with briefcase, was cast
Urban legend has it
Before they shipped
That Colossus to Columbus
A foundry worker
With a profound sense of history
Slipped the newspaper
Full of the Kent State killings
A paper he'd wrapped in plastic
Like a body bag
Into the hollow, Governor's briefcase
Now, he thought to himself
It's sealed in bronze for posterity
That gesture sub rosa
Moved the Jim Rhodes tribute
Beyond the hallowed ground of art
To the status of a time capsule
With a historical judgment
At least equal to that of the pigeons
In the fragrant, Ohio air

## Barbara Tanner Angell

Falling asleep with Barbara
In her forest room, her treehouse
Among the stars, this angel
With the open mouth, her poems
Under the tongue, stored there
Ready to be used as needed, the cool
Jazz sound of the oxygen machine
A slow ride of the cymbal
I assume, assuaging her pain
Chhhhhhhhhhh
I'm there in a half dream
In a sad chair, drowsy after work
Having just signed as a witness her will
I have my wits about me, she said
I know. I'm one of them, I added
Sharing the laughter and now this drifting
In and out, sleepers awakening, startled into dialogue
It's as if we're floating on a stream of language
Past pain's flotsam and jetsam, our bodies submerged
Only the shadows of our voices revealed...
To paint, to write, she muses, the interplay
I define my art by this window before me...
An exit of light, Barbara sails away
Breathless, over her abundance of trees
Real, on canvas, her fox's song, hungry owl
Groping mole and amber cat, all her night music
Rain and April, the call of names
Into the honeyed air of eternity

## October Poem

Through the skin
Of night to the bone
Of the naked heart
The wind's a river
For the forest of women
Standing by the water
Their hair, glorious
In the air, diamonds
Stars, pools of light
Leaf fall, electric hum
The weight of the world
Stacked, bound, waiting
For newspaper shoulders
The approaching headlights
Wet grass, tree-lawn snake branch
The way the way curves
The hand caressing the moment
Silences like a sky, the streets
Paved with the gold of autumn
Fallen heaven's alchemy
Cat crawl, insect bite
Skunk smell, the dense
Presence of houses
Where your friend's
No longer living
Where your friend's
No longer dying
You pass by, step over
The sidewalk's web
The floating room
Coughs in the dark
The deaf child sleeping
Only in your ear
The cricket song
Homeward the shadows move
Your dog shadowing you
The shadow of death remembered
Again the words come, repeat

The crime, the cry, the ubiquity of love
Rainwater in a bowl
Silver tears on a golden leaf

## Quiet as a Star

No beekeeper, hooded and gloved
Can take the sting from death
Nor the love from these streets
Of grief, our nocturnal deeds inviting
An insomnia of strangers. Listen
In the distance the theater of fire
Whose siren cry staggers heaven, whose desire
Is a river of hands reaching out to what...
Lash me to the mast?
Tie me, trembling, to the tree?
Again in the moonlight
I climb the tower
The cupola, the spire
Suddenly a witness
Wings of the Paraclete
Beat against the dark
Taking care in the air
Breathlessly I breathe
O hear my broken prayer
For our ancient mother, Africa
The mask for my own mother
A woman of sorrows
Rooted in the struggle
Who first drew me
To this solitude, this light
Down, cut, down, earthbound
My hands, bleeding
Lead me to sensuous applause
In the mirror of the ear
Vertigo rain, white bones dancing
In the teeth of the wind
A saw of thunder. Now
Falling dreamward
The door of night
Ajar, I lie
My soul and I
Quiet as a star

## Gray Day, White Buildings
*for Edward Durden*


Gray day, white buildings
The Free Stamp has again
Been inked in blood
How many Michael Pipkins
Must be buried in its shadow
By the bureaucracies of hands
Washing each other?
Gray day, white buildings
Chief Wahoo dances in the snow
Cleveland's weather
Is not as cold as her justice
Nor her river as crooked
As her politicians
Death is in the air
Has a chokehold on the city
Gray day, white buildings
We struggle, catch our breath
In another night of sorrow
No sleep, no justice, no peace

## Hiroshima Day in Cleveland, 1995

Cooled by evening's simplicity
The water and I are shimmering
The lagoon beckons in the darkness
To an armada of light
Coming by land through the trees
These annual, August lanterns
Lit by the flames of Hiroshima
Are the work of children
And bear in crayon
Their messages of peace
All gather at the water's edge
Yet, after a ceremony
Go no further en masse
As thought halted
By some creature
From the black lagoon
In reality it's verboten
By mutant landlords
Trustees of the Museum of Art
Who jealously guard
Their liquid assets
O Thoreau, Gandhi, King
O Dorothy Day, we need you
Your spirit of civil disobedience
To turn these lanterns
Into boats of freedom
To keep hope afloat
A black rain
Again falls
On a city
*The Thinker*
Still shattered
Sheds a tear

## Kiloren Night Blue Poet

In the corner
Of my eye
Asleep
In a tear
Dear
Sweet
Vladimir

## The Ghosts of Anarchists
*for Sid and Barry*


The ghosts of anarchists
Are riding bicycles
In Lake View Cemetery
As unemployed poets
Bearded and drunk on leisure
Put away their pens
And pull out their penises
To piss on the obelisk
Of John D. Rockefeller
They pull out their peckers
To pee on John D.
Not because they are so poor
They don't have a pot to piss in
But because John D.
That oil-slick, philanthropic prick
With the thin smile
Beneath the plutocratic hat
And the thin, shiny dime
In his long, bony, Baptist
Grasping, capitalist hand
A coin he'd offer as if it were
A Eucharistic wafer
Through his son and others
Of the same silky ilk
And cold-fish militia mentality
O bloody body of Christ!
Swung low his sweet charity
On Ludlow, Colorado
The gun butt to the skull
The boot in the face, everything
Moving shot up: men dying
Along with chickens and dogs
The women and children in tents
Set ablaze, machine-gunned
Massacred!
All caught in the fiery cave below

Miners and their kin
Served the hard death again
Miners who dared
To stand up and strike
And because his grandson
As Governor of New York
Upholding the family tradition
Put a full Nelson
On Attica...Attica...Attica
Let's run the tape once more
The chopper drops the gas
The marksmen fire
The troops move in
Men who are not beasts
Are cut down like beasts
No hostage, blindfolded
Was as blind as this justice
No knife to the throat
Was as cruel
O pity the women
In the eye of the nightmare
And the children of the brothers
Who died inside
And pity us all
On this rocky road
Victims
Of the Rocky Horror Show
Of those in power

Who have died inside

# The Workingman Goes Home
*for my sister*


My breathing's bad, miss. Quick—the mask
Uncoil the tube, the plastic bag
The world is dying: I'm flying
To my father

How's he doing, Sis? Is this it?
Just to move Dad needs a crew: he sits
A realist toward the dark news
And the pain

Old man's the measure: he grows small
He has hardly any voice at all
His whispered thirst brings us
With tears and water

In the dream he's in the mill
No more bad times, sing flesh and bone
The crane comes, the whistle blows
The workingman goes home

## Stardust

*for Steve Melton*

Again
The dead of winter
Whispering in tongues
The song of grief
On the chill air
These bare, black
Stick-figure trees
Their wild gestures
Of prayer, stark
Against the pink
Of heaven...
The day you died
I was in California
In the Bay area
Walking about North Beach
Wondering whether I was still
On the path that led me here
As a young man...
I flew home, arriving
In time to answer the phone
To learn you were breathless
That the breath had left
Your body, was in the treetops
Waiting like a bird
For the light, for the first
Green leaf of spring
To be transformed once more
And return as life
In the lungs, in the blood
In the deep heart's core
Perhaps I myself
Might breathe you in
And sing...
Steve, you know
It was on James Dean's
Birthday you died
And I imagine you two

Tooling around the city
Together, down these
Gritty, industrial streets
Through neighborhoods of hard lives
Of ancient grandmothers
Their soft voices still sounding young
In kitchens of hot coffee
Fresh bread, good soup
I can see you both
Cool in your shades
Trailing cigar smoke
Joking, swapping stories
Of Indiana and Tennessee
Going into Mitzi's
You introduce Jimmy
Order a White Russian
Head for the green felt
To rack 'em up
To break another heart
Dean calls you back
Needs change for the jukebox
Presses J8, you, L2
You've each picked
*Stardust*
It's on there twice
At that you both laugh
You glance out the window
Utter something I can't quite catch
Grab Jimmy. Someone unlocks
The door. You step out, look up
In the sky. Suddenly
All the human sorry you've felt
Is remembered and forgiven
In a Cleveland second
In the beautiful
Falling snow...

## Rich

*for Elmer Richards*


You have to have a heart
To have a heart attack
Cut open the average tuxedo
You'd probably find
An efficient pump
Keeping a nice, steady cash flow
But a heart sailing by
On a bicycle
At home under the sun
The moon and the stars
As big as all outdoors
As the saying goes
Now *that's* a heart
A heart
No bicycle thief
Can steal...

## Light on the River
### *for Lynn Hunt*


Three-legged
Part Indian
And in pain
I long to travel
Out of the body
To the wilderness
Where the tree
Falls in silence
Where the bear dances
To an unchained melody

I told her in today's politics
You need an environmental name
Like Green, Beach, Summer
In fact her friend
Summer was on the way
To Bank Street to meet her
You mean like Hunt, she said
I laughed, replied
That's an old-fashioned
Environmental name

What do the hunters hunt in the city?
Endangered species crossing the street
She was dragged 130 feet, the paper said
By a fire-engine red Pontiac
I went to the library, took out a book
On the Indian, Pontiac. The book said
He first entered history
At the place that is now Cleveland

I called the detective
Working on the case
Richard Zoss told me
They had a suspected vehicle
Were having paint chips analyzed

Were looking for traces of blood
It was red but not a Pontiac
The spirit of the great Warrior chief
Could rest in peace

At the memorial service I learned
Lynn danced like light on the river
And the river was deep and wide

Even a three-legged
Part Indian mourner
Pondering this
Can forget his pain

## A Valentine
*for Tim*

What made your head
So hard, so hard to carry
You laid it on my heart
Your head, heavy on my heart
Then like our Crane and levy
You left too soon, Calhoun
No more Mozart on a friend's piano
Nor jazz chords nor commandments
Of the Lord, no Father, Son
And Holy Ghost, three bearded
Bards from our own bleak coast
Together on the ward, no moving
Pieces on the board nor the bored
Themselves, at the smoky tables
No fable, alchemy, philosopher's stone
No song from the rake's broken teeth
Nor winter's punch choir of trees
All are silent as thieves
Please. Please. The topic for today
Is simple, Is art a disease?
Once
In the custody
Of the police
You were taken
To a room
With nothing
With poetic justice
You called it
The nothing room
How unlike
Your last room
With everything
Technology
To reach the moon
But you flew away
In your poetic guise

The Nighthawk in the sky
Wounded
Your wings dipped
The last blood-ink fell
A farewell poem
Your valentine
In the snow...

**Death**

Death
Comes in
The Bottle Works, orders drinks, refuses to pay. It's your turn, Mister Haims
Says Death, it's your turn to pay. Eighteen shots later, bullets, not booze
Bill, like his namesake the Kid, lights out on the horse
He's ripped off from Death, rides
Till he crosses the River
Hey, Leon, Old Man
He shouts, Hey Shondor
Billy the Kid's
Come home again
As tough as life
In the wildwest
Night, as tough
As the nails
In his coffin

Billy the Kid
For Bill Haims

## On My Haunches

Well, here I am
The kid who caught
For Local 2265
A million summers ago
On my haunches
Late afternoon
Behind the art museum
Green and quiet
With my dogs
The birds, the breeze
The good life, you know
Joggers jogging
Bicyclists biking
My dog chasing them
Or each other or shitting
The big one, Josh, running over
Barking, scaring some poor guy
Away from a tree
Then pissing on it
Usually we're here under the stars
Around three A.M.: just us, the patrol cars
And my ragman roll of cold-eyed musings
Like when I turned forty, my waist was forty
When I was forty-one, my waist was forty-one
My age and my waist are keeping pace
So when I'm sixty-nine since I'm five, nine
I'll be sixty-nine all ways
Of course I won't be able to perform sixty-nine
Or any interesting number for that matter
One thing I'll be able to do, though
Is throw away my Sohio credit card
I won't need gas; I'll just roll to where I wanna go
Maybe I'll train my dogs to push me along with their noses
It might even become an Olympic event. But right now
Having just read in *Rolling Stone* that women dig ugly men
I'm still ugly enough to sleep with

# Four

## "I Hear a New Beatitude, America"

## Train!

Train!
You've driven your golden spike
Into the dark night of my soul
Train!
You carry my death in the smoky
Breath of your cities
Train!
You're the iron horse, the ironic
Force that's sped up the nightmare
Of history, our genocidal mystery
Train!
It'll be a great day when this wobbly
Depressed hobo poet, riding the rods
Finds you're carrying peace
Train!
Mine eyes have been watching you closely
Train. This is now a new freedom train
The new Swing Low, Sweet Harriet Tubman train
No high noon killers on this train
No death nor internment camp counselors
On this train. This is no bourgeois train
This is the Woody Guthrie-Bound for Glory train
This is the Leadbelly train, the A Train, the A.
Philip Randolph-Pullman Porter train, the John
Coltrane, the Ain't I a Woman-Sojourner Truth train
The Great Day in the Morning Peace Train! Train! Train!

## The Speed of Poetry

Ghost taxis
Vanish like breath
On the cold
Night air
Their only fare
Death
Death
Death
From the pitch-
Black dark
A hesitation of crickets
Listen
Seize the moon
The lost country of night
Its torn flag of sky
Dying stars
All is moving now
To the speed of poetry
All is yours now
Cope

## The Prints of Darkness
*for Kelly Novak*


O where are you
Brooding in the dark
Around a corner of hands
Waiting to touch
Or wave goodbye?
Once I wrote of those
Artists of the street
I know the touch
Of the hustler
Beyond the touch
For I am as much
A poverty's child as she
Playing the sounds
Of the city by ear
What arrogance
What naïveté
To you I simply write
No assassin of the heart
Can match your dark fire
Now
At the café of the poets
All my words are consumed
In an apocalyptic sigh
My lost eyes are turned inward
Against the long night's loneliness
With silence I call out
To your elusive beauty
Wanting only
Suddenly to live

**Your Hair**
*for Cindy MacKay*


Your hair is forest
And lightning
The Niagara River
And the hunter's
Moon, the loneliness
Of wolves...this poem

## Lady Day

Easily swayed
Towards blue
Like the sky
Falling, she sighs
Moves on to what-
Ever new weather
Night and the Street
Bring to her singing
Whether or not
The new is in
The knot of news
It's the knot of the noose
She must unloosen, then
Slip through, hip to
The loop's echo, shadow
And weight, and wait
Till after the gavel
Unravels her fate
To travel the darkness
Crying her heart out
On her rolled-up sleeve
No choices now
On the road of cold shoulders
A voice *noir*
As raw and sad as love and war
For the often soft ear of the world
Those wounded words carried
Almost by dream on the injured air
Always a stone's throw from ground zero
O bird afire
Thou harbinger rising
From the ashes of desire
Lean against the silence and sing

# When the Weather Breaks
*for Michael*


When the weather breaks
When the weather breaks
Our hearts
When the weather breaks
Like a river in our hearts
When our brokenhearted river
Crooked as a politician
Crooked and turning politic
Turns its wings southward again
Its crooked wings again southward
Our river words wing southward turning
All the lies the season calls poetry
All the seasoned lies again called poetry
Flow from me to you anew
Flow from you to me
Flow anew
When the weather breaks
When the weather breaks
When the weather breaks

## Winter Bones
*for Clara Pfister*

When the weather breaks
The winter bones of sleep
And waking
Birds still mirror
The heart's silhouette
Our broken dreams
And theirs becoming song
The beast that licks your face
Leads you astray
Down old mud roads
To where the milk and honey flow
Wild in the thicket
Merry blackberry thief
You go till you drop
In an open field
Gay as a fiddle
Your pockets filled
With Bouncing Bet
In the hardihood of quiet
The tree making wood
You feel at home
You catch the river
In its flux and ease
You apologize to water
You praise the light
God's iron grace
The ubiquitous night
You stroke the stone
O blind mole laboring
In the anonymous earth
Your verse's the dove
I hold to my heart
To heal the wound

## A New Beatitude

Waking to starlight
In a dark season
I hear a new beatitude, America
Listen
Blessed are the homeless
For they shall inherit the street
The sidewalk, the bushes
The cold, cold ground
Whatever falls from heaven
Pennies of rain, of snow
Any spare change of weather
Day-old manna
The donut and the hole
In the donut, the hole in the sock
In the sole of the shoe
And in the cold, cold ground
And O I almost forgot, America
This, too, from you
The cold eye of the stranger...

## The Eagle and the Dove

Once
 in a
  dream
  I saw a
   dule of
    doves in
     mourning
      dress; and
       the doves were
       one dove; and on
        the dove's tongue
         there was a tale;
         and the tale was
          of an eagle and how
           an eagle grew; and the eagle
           grew angry; and out of the
           eagle flew a soft white hand;
          and in the hand there was
         a stick; and the
        stick shook the
       sun; and the sun
      split the earth;
     and the earth
    turned to
   dust;
  some-
 where
a voice was lost, somewhere a dream...

## Love Poem

Sleep
Or do
What you will
My love
I'll be your
Sheet your pillow
Your arms against
The night
Have faith
My hands
Will lie untroubled
Out of sight
Or startled
By your beating heart
Awake
To find love blind
And in that rub
A language
Dark as Braille
Each touch a rush
Each deepening mark
A darker omen
Sleep
Or do
What you will
My love
A thief in moonlight
Comes
To rob love blind

## Women at the River's Edge

When woods turn into words
And the words yellow
Under the sun's thumb
Into pools of dead air
On a dog day in a deaf year
Then women at the river's edge
Their hearts beating wildly
Smash their lives
Without permission
On the blind rocks
Sharpened by the mind's eye
Broken, bred on silence
Their hearts heal in the river's dance
Time and again rising in love's anger
Toward the danger on the map...

## The Day Begins

The day begins
A melancholy white
Bone of light
In the wind's teeth
A glowing row of windows

Turned toward the light
Shoes yawn
Their whiskers twisted
The bed is narrow
The house heavy with sleep

I lie awake alone again
Staying with friends
In the shadow of forgotten dreams
A dead horse sensing
The approaching blow

Alone again bone alone
The only light the windows
Again the wind the white
The fire frozen
I lie in wait for what

## Micheline in Cleveland

Rain and stars
The streets are holy
Today even the sun
Broke through, I say
Do the crime
The crime of art and split
And let me drive
The getaway car
I'm crazy like a fox
At the wheel
I mean, Jack
Let's get lost fast
O I know
You're an original
Cat, a ragged lion
Holding sunlight
In your hands
As you beg off
At the West Side Market
To catch what you
Charmingly call
The light rail
But listen, Jack
Go further
Amscray on the AMTRAK
Take your hat, your sack
Your bags and bagatelles
Those fiery love letters
With those crackling-hot
Snapshots
Of big, mature women
Your singing poems, your
Paintings and your pain
And go. Or stay
Or go and come back, Jack
Rain and stars
The haunted streets
Of ghosts, of shadows

And lo
A crooked moon
I may see as bitter
You say
Smiles down
On its children
These children of light
Who ought to know by now
By heart
Your voice
Your outlaw name

## The Evolution of the Unicorn

what I'm getting
at is
some say it's fitting
that is
if you can't adapt
then you're apt
not to be around
safe & sound
very long
among the strong
what's wrong?
...yes, i guess
maybe strong
may be too strong
let's say
those who survive
are they
still alive today
you know, of course
the unicorn
a crazy horse
a while ago
who owned a horn
he couldn't blow
you didn't...oh
well, it's been said
the reason
the unicorn's dead
this season
is because
by natural laws
he never was
& if you're out
before you bat
that's that

## The Festival of Blind Faith

Day breaks the bones of sleep
My dream sinks like a rock
What time is it?
The eyeball asks the clock
A time for tea and error
Hooray, our eviction notice came
Another package deal
In the lies that pass for news
Lies our obituary
Ah, the decisions some never make
What to do, who to marry
What's the good word?
The ear asks the clock
Tick tock, tick tock
The guns of fun are cocked
Hurry, take a partner, take a part
The festival's about to start
Blind faith
With its blood-soaked pitch
Still woos the broken heart

# Fanatic

Into the room's dark gestures
The skin invites itself again
Into the broken light
The reckless eye zeroes in
Moving toward the window
Open to the moon
Its errant beauty caught
In the tree's calligraphy
This tree where the hanged
Man, our savior, lives
O bitter words uprooted
From the heart's sweet tongue
Carried by the wind's teeth
Biting through the stars
To beyond the sky
To the ear of God, I
Was such a fanatic once
You still are, her voice breaks in
The mirror cracks, blood springs
From the hands and feet
You still are, she says
Wrapping my trembling life
Like a homeless street person
In the blanket of her phrase
A fanatic of the moment

## Earth Poem

No garden of earthly delights
This pleasure ground. For me
This is the old neighborhood
Are the stars out tonight?
The sky is still steepled, today is
My birthday and this park, Lincoln
Is where we'll start our Earth Day
Tree-praise firewalk, an after-
Midnight crawl into the valley
Here my mind and I forever ride
A Rosebud sled of memories
The killer hill of West 11th
All the boys of winter had to try
Gone now with the snow, disappeared
Into the concrete poetry of I-490
Gone, too, the swamp
A sometimes forbidden zone
Of rafts and dumped banana stalks
Where my dog, Buddy, and I
Would wander in the moonlight
Yea, though I walk through the valley
Of the shadow of death...
And in slow exploding daylight
As the war and more stars turned to gold
Georgie Joseph and I'd
Fish out pollywogs for our backyard bathtub
All plopped into the void
Splash! Basho's leapfrog haiku echo...
The Flats has always been a place unto itself
The planet I call, Polluto
With its liquid nitrogen, oxygen
Its mystery of white buildings
Endless boxcars, tracks, trucks, bridges
Acid, smoke, ore boats, riverwords, shortcuts
And O, don't miss Liberty's industrial torch
That almost biblical fire by night
Waving like an embattled flag
Worthy of an anthem. Christ!

What do they put in those drinks at the Literary?
I'm just one of the huddled masses
Yearning to drink free, OK, to breathe free
To break free, to carry our shadow warrior, Death
Through the nocturnal ruderal and wretched refuse
To the Earth for whom we only have eyes
Only broken hands to press the flesh
Only broken tongues to promise
To love is to begin again...

## Dizzy at the Bop Stop
*for Ron Busch*


That black pup
In the basement
Of the Bop Stop
Has officially been
Christened, Dizzy
In my lifetime
That's the second
Canine I've personally
Met and petted
Named after the great
Mister Gillespie
If I had a bullfrog
I'd want to call him, Diz
But if a stray dog
Had sauntered
Into my place
Wearing my face
I'd have tagged him
Junior. However
Dizzy is cool
Eternally cool
The King of Bebop
Having split the scene
His trademark
Bent trumpet
Still a horn of plenty
Those golden notes hanging
Fresh in the air
An urban garden of sound
One of the wonders of the world
Listen. Who's Dizzy?
He's the cat to rival
Even Heaven's Gabriel
I remember
My first time
In the Big Apple

A family trip
A gift to my sister
Class of '55
Younger and hip
Sis took me
To my first jazz club
It was Birdland
And there was Diz...

## Poet in Cleveland
*for Robert Mayer*


Asthmatic breath
Diabetic blood
Arthritic bone
My foxy darling
Truffaut pierced
Heart burst, gone...
Eight years of junkyards
Am I fat or just heavy?
I hang with Hart Crane
Langston Hughes, d.a. levy
Along the Cuyahoga is Poetsbank
We catch fire, give the river thanks
Poems! Poems! Walking at night
In the bathtub, on the phone
My breath, my blood, my bone...

# The Calling

I hook
A pager
To my belt
I fill
My days
With rage
Those in jail
I help
Those in love
I praise
Long ago
Love called
Me home
No, I said
Half-crazed
Then she
Hooked me
To her dark
Jailed me
In her maze

## Theology

God is dead
Killed by the head
Buried in the heart
A childhood part
Preserved in art
A luxury, O Lord
Only the poor
Can afford

## Dirty Pool

*for Truffaut*


Throwing a dog
Who doesn't like water
Into the water
Is like hitting someone
You supposedly love
Once you've done it
They'll never trust you again
And the first chance they get
They'll put the bite on you
You dirty son of a bitch

## Truffaut at Cumberland

Taking up the cause
Of crow, sky is happy
Water on rock's loose sister
To crocodile, black snow
On sidewalk, dogs talk
In short waves of grass
Ants anticipate picnic pleasures
Truffaut & dark dog sniff & split
Hares in hole keep low profiles
Bushy tail is periscope, U.S.S. Squirrel
Whoosh, submarine flies up tree
Feet swarm
Truffaut follows odors
Orange ball spins
Wings heavenward
Blue bicycle boy
Whizzes by, whistling
On monkey bars
Acrobats hang
Banana smiles
Hi, dog, says skateboard
No need for long hair to say
Have a nice day

## Small Tragedies of the Junkyard Poets' Auto Recycling Dog, No Nukes, Pro-Garlic Poetry Festival—
## Sunday, August 7, 1983
*for Myron*


Forty pounds of hot dogs disappear
Seven chairs walk away
The chicken doesn't move
The books don't move
The winning dog, Phineas T. Muldoon
Bites the Master of Ceremonies
The Master of Ceremonies moves
To the Emergency Room at Kaiser
Gusti turns the color of garlic
Has to leave
Alex Bevan, coming since July 7
Never shows
Professional heckler overcharges
Wait till next year

## People with Sad Stories Get in Free

Your attention, please
Your attention, please
Your dog has fleas
My dog's a disease?
Thank you, I think you're strange, too
I'd like to announce a change
In the policy of the house
In order to enhance the value
Or rather, your appreciation
Of what we so recklessly call poetry
From now on when I get up here to read
I'm charging you a fee. You heard correctly
Misters and sisters, no more free readings from me
It's like that old saying I just made up
Give the poets this day their daily bread and water
I mean, their daily bread, and water their garden of verses
Or something like that.
Anyway, If you want me to read to you
You feed me.
Everybody pays.
Well, not everybody.
People with sad stories
Get in free.
This poet's no fool.
I don't want to read to an empty room

## Charlie Chaplin

Charlie followed us
Home one night
Came up the stairs
Like he lived there
At first I didn't
Know who it was
Started muttering names
Tried a few
Then it hit me
This is Charlie
Now I'm told his
Used-to-bes
Know he's with us
Have known all along
And are telling everybody
In the neighborhood
To say nothing
I guess some people
Find it hard
To live with a comedian

## America

*on Maj's 60<sup>th</sup>*

A paradise lost
A pair of dice found
Hang 'em from
The rearview mirror
Shall we go now?
The dogs, the women
Are sleeping...
The heart unfolding
Into a bird on the wing
Asks of Heaven only
For a mouth to sing
Come on, Sweetpea
The motor's running...

## Super Poem
*for Fran and Ted Dostal*


Superman, as you know
Is really from Cleveland
But why call him
The Man of Steel?
He never worked
A day in his life in the mill
And now that these plants are closing
Along with newspapers
Like the *Daily Planet*
Where he did work
Maybe we should call him
The Man of Rust
But listen
Don't worry about Clark Kent
Coming up with the rent
Just with his eyes
He could get a degree
In X-ray Technology at Tri-C
No, Superman never worked in the Flats
Of the Margaret Bourke-White photographs
When Steel made wealth
And the weather of Hell
With its Satanic tail of fire
Fire, Lord, fire that burns the soul
But I do know one steely-eyed
Hell of a worker
The Iron Man of the Left
Red Ted to his friends
Hostile Dostal to his enemies
Who's more powerful
Than the locomotive
That delivered him
From the Deep North
Loco motive, that is crazy reason
Who, faster than a speeding bullet
Can line up people to picket
Fire up a crowd, then with it

Leap like Lenins over the tall stories
The tall propaganda of the bosses
In the tall buildings
That defy the sky
Not with a single bound
But bound to the collective
Is it a burden? No
It's a plain fact, Jack
We don't need Supermen
We need to organize
Ordinary men, ordinary women
Because together we're extraordinary
And Fran—we need a thousand
Like her, needle in hand
Now there's a thousand points of light
To stick it to the capitalists
To needle those butt brains
With shots of Revolution!
In the never-ending battle
Our struggle
We need to speak Truth
To do Justice
But the Man of Steel
That cold, lying bastard
He's just ice
He's not for real
He spends his day
Defending the men who steal
The American Way

## Weeds

In Chicago bars
Everyone's competitive
Poets slam poets, turtles
Race against turtles, women
Wrestle women in jello
And this isn't, Weeds
This is wild onions, wild garlic
It's what Chicago means
In Native American
The wildness that rises
On the prairie tide
The hustling wind
The bright water's edge
Our hearts and words
Exploding like fireworks
Ask any native son
Or daughter. Ask me
I'm no virgin
I've been around
This block before
I'm just down
In the mouth
Over the sizzle
In your brainpan
That lets you forget
The wild night I arrived
Walked up here and knocked
The whole damn crowd on its ear

## Eat Chinese

Come on
Politics is easy
Art is easy
Isn't that right
Mister Binge
Performance Artist
Extraordinaire
Eating up your grant
At the all-night café?
Make the hard choices
You're on the side
Of the murderers
Avoid the hard choices
The murderers applaud
From the front row
The heart
Opens and closes
Like a fist
The fist
Opens and closes
Like the heart
By the way
What do you weigh
By now and
What is Art?
Eat Chinese
Your fortune reads
You're not fooling anyone

## Lost in the Personal
*for Amy Boyer*


Why am I
Lost in the personal?
I never say
Cheese, don't
Shoot fish or first
And ask questions
Later in a barrel
Too easy and slow
To jade, I still
Believe new, clear
Visions. Save me
A place in line
I like your face
And need time
To hocus-focus
Shoot the works
Again. By the way, I

Only have eyes for you

## All About Ronnie

The President of the United States
Once a spokesman for General Electric
And now an advocate of nuclear energy and arms
Has a message for the nation

Ladies and gentlemen
The President of the United States

My fellow countrymen
Eat
Light

## Green Poem

The Sierra Club
Is now Club Sierra
Earth Day is Mirth Day
The looters and polluters
Have given birth to a
Bloody shade of green
Our environmental leaders
Have deserted the banks of the river
And are laughing all the way to the bank
That's where the real green is
It's the old American success story
If you can't beat 'em, join 'em

And the public be damned

## Fighting Words

I KNashed my teeth
In Cleveland Heights
Got a pain in my head
They put me
In the Workhouse
I felt half-dead
Like a timed-release
Aspirin
Bayer got me out
Took away my pain
Put my enemies to rout
Yes, he won my case, Mama
Now it's time to shout
With a wise, crack lawyer
And money from Dad
Justice in America
Ain't half-bad

## The Darkness

The darkness drops again
And who has the courage
To match the cuckoo spit
Out of the nymphs of spittlebugs?
Do you believe in the right to be read
The right not to be dead if you write?
Or is that you, Mr. Hughes, still in the news
Hiding behind the ayatollah's beard?
I knew you were too rich to die
And now Mr. Rushdie is too rich to die
Even I, a poor poet, am too rich to die
And you others
In your sky-high, cornucopian suites
In the towers of your cowardice
Are you too rich to die?
Come down. The winds of controversy
Blow Satanic. Untether your chains
Roll up your sleeves and trumpet the Verses
A la Gabriel over the counter
Over the counterrevolutionaries' gestures of death
Their threats to the artist, the life of the mind
The life of Salman Rushdie
For at the moment he is all of us
He is what we once called, Everyman
And if you are asked, Who is Spartacus?
Say, I am Spartacus
Who is Rushdie?
I am Rushdie

**Cheryl Lessin**


Put on your black armbands
Freedom of speech has died in Cleveland
Do you smell smoke? It's not the flag
Burning. It's the Bill of Rights
They're coming after artists, radicals
They want to change the citizenry
Into good Germans. You're next
The time to resist is long overdue
That's the lesson Lessin has taught us
It's beyond, chilling. We're into the Ice Age
Frozen zombies, night of the living dead
Happy Halloween, folks!

## If You See K-65

*for Thomas W. Appelgate, Jr.*

Why don't you just
Investigate original sin
The beginnings of the nuclear
Family, Adam and Eve
And let the newspapers
Call it, Applegate?
Your latest case, K-65
The original atomic soup
Still on the menu at Fernald
Well, it's like you say
If you see K-65
You probably won't have
To worry about someone
Needing you and feeding you
When you're 65 or 4, 3, 2
One thing is certain, Thomas
Nuclear waste
Is a terrible thing to mind

## We Need a Sign

We need a sign
In the sky, Bless
This space and all
Who enter. We need
A probe of the plutonium-
Powered politics of plutocracy
A lot of p's. We need a lot of
Peace. That's *all we are saying...*
Let us not move from drive-by
Shootings to flyby genocide
That slingshot flyby
Maneuver to lovely Venus
May leave us
In a radioactive flytrap
Tell Cassini
We like high fashion
As much as the next guy
But we just can't do
Launch next week
We'd like to retire
To Florida, not retire Florida
We'll leave that up to Atlanta
And hey, if they need photos of Saturn
Let them see my neighbor
He drives one
But what drives them
To shake hands with the Devil
And put all of us on earth at risk?
We're no longer talking about
Errors in judgment
We're talking about EVIL
EVIL that surpasses even Hitler
EVIL that surpasses all human understanding

## No Business as Usual

*4/29/85*

I died to wake the dead
Wake up, my action said
As down I lied to tell the truth
To save the world. Gravity made me brave
I stayed. To love the earth is to keep
An ear to the ground. I found
What goes round comes round
My decision? We need a new, clear vision
The dead are lovely in the street
Their hearts beat, and their lips repeat
Don't tread on me

## Hieronymus Bush

Does Barbara's Rough Rider, our road warrior
Hieronymus Bush, when not dwelling
On his version of the new world order
Share our déjà vu vision of Hell, the long
Nightmare of a quicksand trap as he plays God
And his God-awful game of Gulf
On the Persian rug in his Oval Office
Sending his Nintendo Luftwaffe
His Desert Storm Troopers over there
To raise sand, to rock the cradle
Of civilization, to bomb the Garden of Eden?
He's taken his fellow Americans hostage
In this new Babylonian captivity
But is he really so damn mad
At Saddam for giving him the chance
To kick ass in the mother of all battles?
I bet he shakes up the sheiks
Aren't they wondering in their secret hearts
Whether he'll make a desert out of their desert
Blow away every oasis, smoke every camel?
Will the Euphrates flow through Hades?
O Tigris, Tigris, burning bright
In the rockets' red glare, in the oil-
Wellian night...bombs bursting in air
Look! Stars over the desert. Listen...
Wish I may, Bush is praying, wish I might
Body Baghdad Hussein tonight
Prove our improved might is right...
Or will it only prove our Hitler
Is bigger and better than their Hitler?
We hit with high-tech, high-five precision
We're not just bombing Iraq. We're bombing
Hard places, bad people, the inner cities
Of America, our minorities, our homeless
Our victims of the plague, AIDS, the future
Of our children, abandoned, unschooled
What are their options? Join up and die

Or eat dope and die? Where is hope?
Hope's over there entertaining the troops again
And again war is hell, even when sanitized
By the military. War is censorship. War is prison
For dissenters. War is Abraham cutting Isaac's throat
The ram scrammed. The goat never showed
Call me Ishmael, Melville wrote. Is America
Moby Dick, the global swing of the nightstick
The unholy nine yards and the rose that's sick?
Mother, forgive us. Father, forgive us
Sister, forgive us. Brother, forgive us
Husband, forgive us. Wife, forgive us
Daughter, forgive us. Son, forgive us
Earth, forgive us. Air, forgive us
Fire, forgive us. Water, forgive us
And wash our hearts clean
Let us grieve...and love
And begin again...

## A Prayer from Brother Swinger

Let us pray
For poor Jessica
Trapped
In a motel
With an evangelist
Please send money
To save her
From being
Bored again
And now that
Religion is politics
And the saved
And the unwashed
Are part and parcel
Heart and bar stool
Of the same fanatic mix
Let us pray
For the ward heeler
And the faith healer
Let them heal
Their own faith
Before it's too late
And they end up
In the Lord's
Emergency ward
Let them not OD
On G-O-D or G.O.P.
Which rhymes with money
Which you send, Amen
Not to them but me
Brother Swinger
God's gossip and Gospel singer
Here with the latest word
Hallelujah, praise the Lord
We accept Mastercard...

# The New Love Song of J. Alfred Prufrock
*for Lawrie Mott*


J. Alfred walking on the beach
The bottoms of his trousers rolled
Asks himself as he grows old, grows old
Do I dare to eat a peach?
If peaches were mermaids and could sing
Wouldn't Prufrock be shocked
To learn a thing or two
About pesticides' residue?
Their song would certainly say
Stay cautious and wash us

In the fields the growers come and go
Spraying Rampage, Lambast, Bronco

O Captan, my Captan
That's not the Parthenon
That's Parathion
And Benomyl
Has a special skill
Unlike the rest
It can hide
From a routine test

In the fields the killers come and go
Spraying Modown, Tough, Pounce, Turbo

Carbaryl, Dicloran
Endosulfan
Yes. Pesticide is suicide
On the installment plan
O, true love, Prufrock
All these toxins surround us
Wake, wake...and act
Lest they drown us...

In the killing fields they come and go
Spraying Prowl, Submerge, Torpedo

## Love & Carriage
*for Pam*


Hot type
The keys are waiting
A ribbon of beach
A backspace
Out of reach
Of whatever it is
That wishes
To white us out
Call it Cleveland
Call it
Eternal winter
The cold shift
Closing in
On the margins
Of the soul
Let's lock it out
Put it on the index
Off it, delete it
Press on
Forget the asterisk
On to the ampersand
To eyes, starry
Ringing bell, to
Flash of your fingers
Shaping my poem

## Rock Court

The air is the court
Of last resort. Trade oak
For Toyota, maple for Saab
Ash for Jaguar, poplar
For Olds, you're trading
Your life, your breath
For smoke and mirrors
Don't betray yourself
Don't betray the land. Live
Live it up. And let the trees
Live it up, too, from root to star
From darkness to light. Go
Find elsewhere to park your car
Stand here on this height
On this rock and let these trees
Stand for your soul
Let there be this place of beauty
From which you can always
Hang your enemies...

## The Electric Pencil Sharpener

My moustache takes its bath
In coffee black as night
That left my room too soon
Somewhere a forest fell
That I might have the news
Come round
With the morning light
And so you see
The sound of the tree
Is heard by the faraway eye
Now Jesus was a carpenter
Who saw the light and sang
And me
I plug my word sword in
An electric pencil sharpener
And every napalm sun day
As men celebrate mass murder
As they grunt like pigs
In Latin, *Vi et armis*, at the altar
I scribble, thrust, and parry
I scrawl to touch on target
Exaltation wall zen
Motherwit graffiti
Bearded jazz prayer doggerel
O ixnay of delight

## The Land of Snow

Many years ago
In the land of snow
Cold snow
She met a man
Who took her hand
Cold hand
He took her hand
And bid her blow
The cold cold
From the snow
She blew the cold
As hot as hell
The music fell
And froze as well
It never rose
Till she rubbed
His nose and so
You've been told
And now you know
If it's cold
In the land of snow
And you go
How to make love
Like an Eskimo

## Tits Delaney

Tits Delaney
Finally lands a job
Running Irv's bar during the day
I congratulate her, Some of my best friends
Are behind bars, I tell her. Tits Delaney in-
Creases her cleavage and her tips, gets extremely
Pushy, even with old friends. Being one of the oldest
I, of course, protest. You think you're the big bos...boss
Around here, don't you? You're just the titular head
Tits turns, zeroes in on me with that killer pair
Of eyes. Are you orderin', she says, or are you
Loiterin'? That's Tits, alright, always quick
With a quip that goes right for the jugular
She could keep this job
A long time

## The Blue Circle
*a T-shirt poem for Pat*


One night
On Lorain Avenue
I met this wino
I was outside
The Blue Circle
Waiting to read
We liked each
Other's T-shirts
And traded right
On the spot
He gave me his
Robinhood Fire Chief
I gave him my
Junkstock
A 24 hr. arts marathon
In a junkyard
Later he went inside and
Dangerously sang a song
He seemed to make
Everyone uncomfortable
He got the crowd hostile
Fired up, you know
Ready for poetry...
Now I'm trading again
This time for one that says
Razzle Dazzle
The given name
Of my dog, Razz
Killed in West Virginia
Autumn, '76
By a young patriot
Going to a fire...

## My Last Poem

Here's my latest
I give it to you
To my but not your surprise
There's nothing on the paper
I even look on the other side
Where have the words fled to?
You smile and say
That's the best thing you've ever written
You've never liked what I write and I
I keep as silent as my last poem

## Within the Brightening Fire I Sing

Within the brightening fire I sing
Call me by my righteous name
We'll choose ourselves and grow old
With no holds barred and turn away
From win and lose the bars on the love we hold
We'll choose ourselves and rejoice and grow together
And grow old and turn away from win and lose
As down the darkling hole we fall O call us by
Our righteous names within the brightening fire I turn
And sing grow old with no holds barred and no bars
On the love we hold as down the darkling hole we fell
We chose our names ourselves grew old together in
The brightening fire the darkling hole we fall we sing
The names we hold together grow rejoice and turn away

## 3 AM

Not the quiet fire of Sinatra
In the wee small hours of the morning
No, what works its magic now
Is of Chinese origin. Swoosh. Pop. Pop. Pop
Poet Mark Hopkins and candidate Bob Lanigan
Who just ran again, are shooting off fireworks
Good Catholic boys turned bad, turned
Gunpowder anarchists on the streets of suburbia
Crack. Crack. Swoosh, Roman candles, lady fingers
Bursting into flames, into flowers of evil
A devil's prayer in the ear of our Lord
In the long ear of the law
Is there a problem, officer?
Don't insult my intelligence
How'd you like to be awakened
Three in the morning by this racket?
The man in blue confronts the poet who
An eye on his watch, acknowledges *tempus fugit*
But, in point of fact, informs the officer
It's not three in the morning
It's two twenty-three
That's it, fumes the heat
You really want this ticket, don't you?
O Poor Mark, another poor mark
On the report card of life
Is Gerard Manley spinning in his grave?
In their pre-fourth, Francis Scott Key
Exuberance our celebrants forgot
F. Scott Fitzgerald's warning
His word to wise guys
In a real dark night of the soul
It is always three o'clock in the morning

## Often I Imagine

Often I imagine myself
In the early evening
After the workaday world
Has come home and eaten
The dishes still on the table
Cigarettes and coffee, maybe even
Company over, conversation between
An old friend and the woman with whom I live
Music on the radio, the noise
Of other households settling down
The muted sounds of traffic moving
Perhaps in the sky a bird, a jet...
Often I imagine
In this very ordinary situation
And pleasant time
Going into the bedroom
Lying down
And blowing my fucking brains out

## Now the Road

On the walks
Where children play
Lay the broken
Vertebrae
As the grass
Where lovers laugh
Shaped my windy
Epitaph

Now the road
Winds round
The heart
Both are old
And both are dark

# Hair

What a disgusting habit!
Pulling out my hair
Is it sexual?
Can't keep a beard now
Nor moustache nor sideburns
Hair disappearing everywhere
Head, chest, armpits, crotch
Even those damn dingleberries
Have nothing to cling to
And my friends!
What must they think
After each visit
Little piles of hair around the chair...

Ah, but look at it this way, Daniel
The whole world will be happy
When you're bald

## Want and Like

You just never take
The world seriously
You only want
A safe place to play
Your dangerous game
What is it you call it
Art? I understand
I'd like to be invisible, too
But not locked
In the shadows
And the key
Thrown away

## Bridges

Betrayed
Dumped
Lovesick
I'm thinking
Of suicide
I'm thinking
Suicide's
A good excuse
To jump off
The Main Avenue
Or the High Level
Or the Hope Memorial
All these
Childhood bridges of mine
Spanning the Cuyahoga
Undecided
(The name originally
On my birth certificate)
I use these Ors
To reach the bank
Where poets
Schooled in darkness
Read
To lovers
Due to leap

Their voices
Span
The darkness
Like a bridge

## Justice
*for Lesley Brooks Wells*


Who is justice for?
Just us, the privileged
And just ice for the poor
Surely where there's ice
There's human desire for fire
For fire is heat and light
Light for the darkness
Of the pale woman, blind-
Folded, holding the scales
And heat for the icy heart
O let its waters flow
From brooks, wells, rivers
To the sea, a flood of love
Till even the very stone
That surrounds us cries out
Mercy...Mercy...Mercy

## The Silence of the Cranes

Who finds
In the wild
Darwinian blue
An avian heir
Of the dinosaur
That savior's egg
Cracked open
Wing and prayer
Would keep along
Our own
Industrial shore
The immense, black
Silence of the cranes

What lets us praise
We pray for now
The endangered
The water, the steel
The silence
To speak our history

## The PCB Sparrow
*for Kim Hill*


Keeping my vigilance eternal
For the catcher of outlaw dogs
I let Truffaut run free in d. a. levy park
As I plumb the depths of the morning paper
Having come to the edge of Arabican ambience
To join the few, the proud
Those who wait out the decaffeinated coffee drought
Suddenly a sparrow tweets a greeting
Hey, Street Poet, how's Truffaut?
Do I know you? I ask as he lands on the comics
According to the latest pole, he continues
I mean the one I just left across the road
From Coventry Books, in case of emergency or spill
When those PCBs are set free from their Pandora's box
You're to call the Coast Guard.
CEI imagines you Coventry folk
Are so high, you can read the warning at bird's-eye level
The only reason I'd call the Coast Guard, I tell him
Would be to find out whether the coast is clear
You make sure your head is clear, he snaps
And mind your own PCB's wax. Here's the facts
We are boxed in from sea to shining sea
I sing the box electric. Thirty-five million of them
Each offering our salad days a dressing
Of oil and toxic PCBs
You won't hear them ticking but they're time bombs
A hundred in this area explode every year
If only they all had silicone which is safe
But you know how slowly the corporations move
When it's costing them money. Let me put it this way
Cancer, cardiovascular disease, liver damage, abdominal pain
Skin lesion, reproductive failure, nervous disorder
Respiratory...
OK, OK, I say, I'll give the Coast Guard a call
I can just see the USS Cod coming up Coventry
Rescuing all the alkies who sit illegally on Irv's planter
Saving their livers from PCBs

And what of the lovely Dylan Thomas poets
You who have adventures in the skin trade
Reading in public, Bird adds
It's alright to be fat and read
But with bad skin from PCBs
Forget it. You'd better only publish
O phone pole ringed
With poisonous fruit, I emote
What a joke you play on us
You spill. You stay. You grow. You leak
There's a mad dog loosed in Eden
And nowhere to flee
O AT&T, O PCB, O CEI, O CIA
O spare us, says Sparrow and flies away
Looking for a clean, organic tree
As Truffaut runs by, barking goodbye
Headed for the same tree

## The Sky is Blue

Happy as our beast
We arrive home
The war's over
Our enemies have fallen
From high places
The rent's paid
We're nobody's fool
We take the happiness
We can handle
We know
Behind the tree
Between the buildings
In the doorway
On the beat
A Peace Officer waits
Ready to wage war
To bust us again
For jaywalking
You've got me, I'll say
Don't bother to check
Officer, I admit it
From an early age
Yes, a record
Of disorderly convictions
Of...
I know you, he'll say
You're the poet
The sky is blue
Fuck you

## The Night the Corrigans Burned Down St. Colman's

I have nothing to say about the night
The Corrigans burned down St. Colman's
Judge not and you shall not be judged
Has always been my way
But when you have that many
Celebratory candles lit
You have to be fit, in shape, not winded
Nor blowing it out the other end
And when it comes to wishing
You can't be silly and hesitate
Shilly-shally like Hamlet until it's too late
Even with a firefighter in the family
You don't tempt fate
No, no, I have nothing to say
About the night that mob of grinning
Corrigans burned down St. Colman's
Save, maybe, for wishing they live
To do it again and

Let them eat cake

**O**

O
that this
book were still
a tree so I could see
the poet who would've written

s

w

i

f          n

r

o          g

m

i

t

## The Girl Who Dyed Her Hair

Once upon a tick tock
In the land of You & Me,
Otherwise known as Us,
And sometimes U.S.A.,
There lived a girl who dyed her hair:
Some days blonde,
Some days red,
Some days brunette,
And some days back to black,
But always she was blue.

"I'm so bored," she would say, "I don't know what else to do." So she thought and thought, but it all came to naught...till suddenly out of nowhere, as she rubbed her lucky rabbit's foot, she got this idea:

"Why don't I go in the woods, ask a rabbit to be my friend, and take him home with me?" So she went to the woods, found a hole and what do you know? Out popped, or rather, out hopped a rabbit.

"Is your name Peter?" she asked.

"Naw," said the rabbit, "and it ain't Bugs neither."

"My goodness!" said the little girl, not so surprised at a talking rabbit but by the way he talked.

"Robert's the name," said the rabbit as he thumped the ground. "What's yours?"

"My name's Peggy," the little girl said.

"Oh yeah," said the rabbit getting excited, "You know Whole Hog and His Five Little Piggies? Used to be at Farmer Brown's. Then off they went to Chicago. Ain't heard no news since. Guess 'Ole Whole' got himself a job and is too hog-tired to write."

"My name's Peggy," she giggled, "Not Piggy. You better call me Peg so you won't get mixed up again."

"Peg's a nice name," said the rabbit, "I'd hang onto it if I were you."

"Of course I will!" said Peg, "A name's a gift our parents give us and I always keep all their gifts. Just like this ring. See." And she showed him the gold ring her parents had given her on her last birthday.

"That ring's a pretty thing," said the rabbit

"Why thank you, Robert," said Peg. "It's fourteen Karat, you know."

"Fourteen carrots!" shouted the rabbit, "Now you're talking my language. I sure wish I had fourteen carrots right now. That'd really make me happy."

"Well," said Peg, "I can make you happy. If you come hop-hop-hopping home with me, I'll give you all the carrots you can eat."

"Wow!" said the rabbit. "Let's go!"

So Robert, the rabbit, went home with Peg and liked it so much he never wanted to leave. He had all the carrots he could eat...and more. For pretty soon the people of Us saw a little girl with a rabbit.
Sometimes both were blonde,
Sometimes brunette,
Sometimes red,
And sometimes black,
Or the girl would be blonde
And the rabbit red,
Or the girl a brunette
And the rabbit yellow,
Or the girl a redhead
And the rabbit brown,
Or...Or...Or...
Anyway, it was always a surprise
And even today they still talk about
The little girl who dyed her hare.

## Tavern Poem
*for Martin*

In the barking spider dark
Where angels speak
And the old lion echoes
The fire's roar, his tale
Told and told again
Among the youth
The dead rose
Light as the pale moon
The moon's news
Yellowed with age
Now all lie together
Downwind below
The fallen, broken sky

## Potlatch

La Charity
Begins at home
Bucks the jetstream
Arrives like Halloween
A white chocolate bar
With a razor blade inside
And the Cheshire Cat
And the Mona Lisa
And the smiley face
All lose their shit-eatin' grins
And the moon is blood-red
As the Cuyahoga flows
Into a slaughterhouse
Of honkie, middle-class Kumbha
And all the dogs in town go mad
Poem at the mouth, barking
Ralph! Ralph! Ralph!

## The Dog Barked

The dog barked
The money ran out
What passions drove
Naked pedestrians
(Filled the street with feet)
The bestial Blue went wild
All shimmied starward
This is what happened
Woke up the moon
Hid in the trees
The car-studded night
Unable to bear the traffic
And what grows on top of them
Luckily, the bite matched the bark
Toward the talk among the leaves

## Outpostscript
### A Spontaneous Love Poem

Hairy asshole, Wolfman, ofay poets
Blowing up the ghettos of your suburban minds
Who needs the shit that runs from your
Hallowed-hollow-hollywood mouths?
Fuck you, you still unborn mothers
Just give me some of the shit you get high on
And I'll find my own way of saying Yes, No, Maybe, Now, Wow
Even Stephen, the first Christian to get stoned
Would be turned off by you
Yet still, I think you *look* beautiful
And though you don't blow my mind
In your honor I'll blow my nose

## A Dark Surprise

Bitter
Butterfly
My heart
Longing
For its cocoon
A dark surprise
What was once
So displeasing
Brings beauty
To the eye

## The Birds of Paris
*for George Hrbek*


Lighthearted
Long ago
In the City of Light
The birds singing
I throw my arms
Round a tree
Barbara says
I wish you'd
Hug me
Like that
Now
Though I've
Grown old
Barbara cold
Back home
In the City of Trees
Every time my friend
George hugs me
Or someone else
Like that
That lights
The heart. Again
The birds of Paris
Sing...

## Miasma

Meow, say tongues
When cats catch up
With them. Cat got mine
And more, got throat frog
Got lung fish, got bird breath
I sink in miasma and gasp, grasp
The heartstrings of my fellow sufferers
Wheeze the people allergic
Pussy feathers, duck dust
Poland, uh, pollen
We cough our days away
Tap our feet to a ragweed beat
Grin and barely endure till Theo Dur
Or sometimes in that airless hell
I, I, Isuprel...Aahh sss hupp
Cough CoUgh cOuGh
CoUgH coUgh couGh
CoUgh CoughH coUGh
COugh coUGH cOFF
Ahhh another PHLEGMboyant
Asthma attack over wow

## Ground Zero: Downtown Cleveland


At ground zero the Terminal Tower is terminated
The Soldiers and Sailors Monument goes AWOL
The Sohio Building says, Sayonara, goes from full serve
To no serve in a short-lived moment
Trials at the Federal Building are postponed
All library fines are cancelled; the Public library is cancelled
At the Free Speech Quadrant the statue of sedentary Mayor
                                        Tom L. Johnson
Is moved for the last time; there is no Free Speech Quadrant
Moses Cleaveland makes a landmark decision, packs up his
                                        Pedestal
And flies the coop with his pigeons; Pigeon Mary is out of
                                        business
All traffic at Public Square is re-routed through China by way
                                        of Hell
Straight down through a 300 ft. deep chuckhole
Local 1099, representing laborers for the Division of Streets
Immediately goes out on strike, demanding more health
                                        benefits
And hazardous duty pay. Along with other pedestrians
I lie down in the street at Ontario and Euclid and pretend
                                        to be alive
I am not arrested by the SWAT Team. There is no SWAT Team
There is no street. There is no 1. There are no pedestrians
There is only a pulverization and a crater 1200 feet in
                                        diameter
By now it is obvious to everyone...the poetry has gone out of
                                        our lives

# Eulogy for Daniel

Pay my respects
To life, to death
And give my heart's
Breath to the green wood
The fallen rock
The roadwork ahead

(from **Kentucky Luck**)

- - -

## Up the Stairs I Rise to Wake the Moon:
## Eulogy, Daniel Thompson's Funeral,
## Church of the Covenant, Cleveland, Ohio,
## May 10, 2004

Daniel was, for years, a puckish and welcome intruder in our house in Kent, a first story man. My wife LuAnn would sometimes look up from her reading or work at hand and say, *I think Daniel is coming to visit.* He would barge through the door unannounced, unbidden, like one of D.H. Lawrence's strange angels. *Admit them, admit them,* urges Lawrence in his poem. Admit him, we did, gladly. I never got past the bright map of his face, though I do recall he always stomped into the house, a bow legged twostep. His face, an impish grin as if he had let the air out of one of my tires or picked all of the preacher's tulips or committed a misdemeanor for love or justice or both. He arrived hungry. He couldn't eat everything because of his diabetes, but he ate all of everything else, with lip smacking, polishing the plate with bread gusto. Then, the stories would start. Half the people Lu and I didn't know in his Damon Runyon/Mickey Spillane/Dostoevski/Cleveland intrigue epics. We listened, not for the facts or the cavalcade of pilgrims in progress, but for whatever it was that moved Daniel, made him rise up in delight, whatever was behind those words like a bee swarm round his head.

In the poetry of Virgil, we find the phrase *lacrimae rerum,* the tears of things, an old and abiding pity, what brokenness knows deep in the chest. Daniel always understood that there are tears inside everything, even words. Especially words. Daniel knew that words are also full of honey. Honey and tears are the marrow of words. Daniel, the poet of tears. Daniel, the poet of honey. Daniel, the poet of vinegar and salt. Daniel, big whiskered wooly hummingbird, found ways everyday to drink from the moment's source, the orange trumpet vine, the blue morning glory, the sweet pea blossom, the rose with petals of concrete, the rusted sunflower.

The first night after Daniel stepped into the shadows, Lu and I lit candles, in mason jars, and set them out on the front steps. I couldn't shake the thought of Daniel flying overhead, circling the earth, unfettered, tumbling like an otter, paddling along on his back, cracking oyster shells with a rock, eating the poems he found inside, pitching the shells down to earth—check your backyard—playing in the Aurora Borealis surf, doing loop-de-loops through the magnetic static of the Van Allen belt, a swimmer in the waning moonlight. Sustained, safe, in the long orbit which cradled him. These candles are navigation lights, little lamps of grief, votive flames of gratitude, little bonfires of love and friendship, landing lights on the deck of the mothership, Krishna's chicory eyes, a constellation in the sky beneath our feet, little tongues of fire making words in the darkness. Light a candle tonight before you sleep your own little death. Set it out under the open sky for the freedom train flyer. Guide him home. All things are an exchange of fire: fire to fire; naked heart to naked heart.

The body is a temporary home. There are only things continually arising and passing away, as is their nature. Everything is preparing to disappear. If you understand this, your heart will ease. Love hard. Pay attention. Be grateful.

As Daniel lay in the hospital bed, Cleveland Clinic, Wednesday afternoon, May 5, Cinco de Mayo, the day before he left, I held his hand and watched his labored breathing beneath the oxygen mask for a couple of hours, the rise and fall of his chest. The abode of his loving heart. Where is breath before we breathe it? If we understand that, we are home. Daniel is going home. In his poems, he mapped the way, blue highways, asphalt, gravel, dirt lowways, a footpath. From there on, it is unmarked. We walk shoeless in the dark. Our homesickness is our guide. Trust that. If you were homeless, you'd be home right now, right here.

Daniel has gone away. No one knows where away is. It may not be far. Away may be no more than the space between two breaths, two heartbeats, or two words, like food, love, home, sing.

Farewell to the poet who kept the watch with the saints in the city and weathered the midnight air.

Farewell to the poet who played the flute cut from articulate bone, music that flowed like a stream of light.

Farewell to the poetry fool who did persist in his folly till he became wise. Few have gone as far down that unmarked trail as Daniel did, hauling the dark cargo of the heart.

Farewell to the poet who wrote his valentine in the ghost snow, who knew that anguish is still the world's official language.

Farewell to the beekeeper stung by death, to the poet who made honey of old failures and regrets. Each poem is a jar of that honey. Each taste carries a blessing, even if hidden. O taste and see.

Farewell to the poet whose question has gone unanswered: *O America, cold machine in high fever/ Why must you devour the young?*

Farewell to the poet who knew, even when lost, there are small dark eyes loving him in secret.

Farewell to the poet who slept under the map of the world and kept time by the heart worn on his sleeve.

Farewell to the poet who shouldered the burden of love's loneliness and taught himself how to live, mouth to hand, hand to mouth.

Farewell to the poet who taught us again and again that the most sublime act is to set another before you.

Farewell to the poet who had the picture of Jesus in his face, who stood like a tree by the water and would not be moved.

Farewell to the poet who sang to the lone sparrow caught in the thicket.

Farewell to the poet who knew we all share one loneliness and one need to break bread and out of that broken silence tumbles everything.

Farewell to the poet who was singular in his disturbance, whose dreams cut like a knife.

Farewell to the poet who was one with the dumb and stood up for the stupid and the crazy.

Farewell to the poet whose cock and bully days are done yet his heart, still shining, sings.

Farewell to the poet who left a trail of breadcrumb words for the alphabet birds that follow us all.

Farewell to the poet who knew we all save coupons no one will redeem except in darkness. Sorrow. Sorrow. Sorrow.

Farewell to the poet who drank the bitter dregs of Winesburg in the dark laughter of rain.

Farewell to the nocturnal poet who stepped through the crack, before dawn, Thursday morning, May 6, not into the heartless dark but into that cornucopia of light for which he yearned.

Farewell to the poet who this day comes to ground zero, upon the down of earth to rest.

Farewell to the poet who waited sixty nine years for the weather to break. This day the weather has broken like a river in our hearts.

O listen to the silence and the words
And the silence and the words and the silence
And the words and the silence...and the words
And the silence.

Fare thee well and safe passage to Daniel whose name
we call out into the honeyed air of eternity. Daniel. Now,
quiet as a star.

Maj Ragain

## Acknowledgements (continued)

Some of these poems have been published in the following: *Artcrimes; Bread, Peace, and Land; Cityscape; Clevebland Rag-O-Zeen; Cleveland Anthology; The Brady Book; The Cleveland Beacon; the Cleveland Edition; The Cleveland Reader; The Cleveland Review; Cleveland Speaks; Coffeehouse Poetry Anthology; The Coventry Reader; 8 Poems By Two; Everyman; A Gathering of Sundays; The Heart's Cargo; The Homeless Grapevine; Jawbone Open; the Jerry's Diner Book; Little Albert; Nature: Pocket Poems; Ohio Police; The Plain Dealer; Plain Press; Pudding Magazine; Sattvas Review; The Second Cleveland Anthology; Seven Poets; Shelly's; Split City; Split Whiskey; Taproot; The Vegetable; Voices in Concert; Voices in Cleveland; Women Speak Out for Peace and Justice.*

*Genetic memory*, a CD, Daniel reading with percussionist Sam Phillips, was released in 1990.

*Under the Map of the World Where I Sleep*, a CD, recorded in Verviers, Belgium, Daniel reading with the percussion group Drumplay, was released in 2002.

*Famous in the Neighborhood.* a film by Gail and Eric Buchbinder honoring Daniel, was released in 2006.

Breinigsville, PA USA
11 April 2011
259593BV00001B/5/P